KT-574-096

CONTENTS

PREFACE

Once upon a time the private sector career norm for those starting out was to join a company or firm and to remain an employee rising through the ranks, probably to retirement. Of course, there were exceptions: the professions, where accountants and lawyers went on to take up positions in industry; and qualified tradesmen who set up on their own or joined a relation in established self-employment. But, on the whole, the pattern of a career lifetime with a single employer did not fracture until the 1960s.

Today the picture is completely different. Regular job-hopping is commonplace and job security is conspicuous by its absence. More and more people each year elect to take self-employment or start their own companies. In 2017, there were 5.7 million small and medium-sized businesses in the UK, representing 99.3% of the private sector; 4.3 million, of which 3.8 million were sole traders or partnerships, employed only the owners.

The decision to go it alone may be taken at any point in the career cycle by:

- Mid-career managers and those with defined skill sets fed up with the daily grind
- Those suffering redundancy or who see no promotion path

- Those choosing to take early retirement and begin again
- Retirees wanting or needing to supplement their pension incomes

Of individuals in these categories few are natural entrepreneurs with the temperament and mind set for assured success and it is for them that I have written this short handbook. Either way, when you launch your business you will be in good company. The book is not intended for school and university leavers who have no taste for entering the job market. For them, self-employment involves a rather different set of decision criteria.

During three decades of self-employment after a first career in industry and with non-executive directorships of a handful of start-ups, I have accumulated more than my fair share of successes and failures. In this book I offer you an introduction to the opportunities and risks that lie ahead, a few cautionary tales and assessments based on that experience.

Jonathan Reuvid

1

TAKING THE PLUNGE

HAVE YOU GOT WHAT IT TAKES?

*"I shot an arrow into the air,
It fell to earth, I knew not where."*

– Henry Wadsworth Longfellow (1807-1852)

At first sight working for yourself is an alluring prospect, but you should take a reality check before you embark on the adventure. Disabuse yourself up front of some popular preconceptions:

- *My time will be my own*
  Not really true. You may not be bound by the tyranny of fixed office hours but there are time-consuming activities to which you will have to attend now that you are no longer supported, such as invoicing and debtor chasing, bill paying and credit management. How best to manage your time is discussed later.

- *I shall be my own master*

  Yes and no. You will certainly be taking the decisions without deferring to a boss but that may be a mixed blessing if you have no collegiate support. You will be subject to the oversight of your bank manager (probably a computerised monitoring system with little recourse to a human decision maker). Above all, since you no longer receive a salary, you will be focusing on cashflow (see chapter 4) which has an authority of its own.

- *I won't have to work with people I don't respect or like*

  Only partly true. If you are employing staff, the choice is certainly yours. But you will still have to deal with difficult customers and suppliers where relationships matter. You will also want to take advice from time to time and you will probably consult only with people you find compatible. That can be a mistake; critical comment from people you don't like, and who probably don't much like you either, may be more valuable.

- *I can take holidays and time off when I want*

  You must be joking. For clients or customers who have an urgent need "I'm taking a few days off" is an inadequate response to demands for your personal service when there is no colleague as substitute. Going on leave whenever you want is a great way to lose business. While lifestyle books pushing for running a business on a few hours a week are in fashion, the reality for most start-ups is very long days and evenings.

Starting your own business with any prospect of success requires a particular mindset, quite different from that of a well paid employee in an organisation, whatever the role or level of responsibility. For many, independence is an uncomfortable suit of clothes. Perhaps the decision to go it alone is easier for a school or university leaver without employment experience for whom the question is primarily one of entrepreneurial instinct.

And so, before you even start to define the business product or service you might provide, make an honest and thorough assessment of yourself as a business person. You might make a balance sheet of your personal attributes, identifying your strengths as assets and your weaknesses as liabilities. Be sure to include the more nebulous qualities such as foresight, patience and persistence – they may be assets or liabilities depending on who you are.

Next, show your balance sheet to your domestic partner if you have one and invite comments. The person with whom you share your private life and home will know the "real" you better than anyone else and will not shrink from gentle and, hopefully, constructive criticism. In any case, it's important to consult your partner, sooner rather than later, on your plans for taking the plunge. You will be counting on them for support and tolerance of changes in lifestyle, perhaps on participation if you go ahead. If you don't have a domestic partner, consult with a close friend or relative who you know will give you their honest and valuable thoughts.

If the personal assessment is unfavourable, think again carefully about giving notice to your employer and review your reasons for wanting to leave. What are the causes for dissatisfaction with your job or the company you work for? Perhaps they can be remedied by changes in what you do or structures within the company. And if that is not possible, consider looking for a fresh challenge in another company, capitalising on your skills, strengths and experience. The aim of this book is not at all to dissuade you from the path of self-employment or business start-up; if you remain determined to follow that course, this is the last time that I shall caution you to think again about your direction of travel.

DOES YOUR PRODUCT OR SERVICE HAVE TRACTION?

Now that you remain steadfast in your resolve, you need to convert any vague feelings about the service or product you have in mind and around which you want to build a business into a precise definition of what you would offer and why it would appeal to potential customers. In the terminology of those who provide funds for new businesses, this is a definition of "concept".

For any concept to fly it needs to have elements of a unique selling proposition (USP). In his book *Business Plans that Get Investment*, David Bateman offers an excellent summary of factors that can provide a USP from which I will borrow five; at least one will hopefully relate to your concept:

- Improvement on an existing product or service
- Specialisation in a specific area or niche within an existing sector
- Cheaper/more cost-effective solution than an existing offering
- New product innovation, patent protected
- First-mover advantage in your country or region (i.e replicating a product or service that exists elsewhere in the world)

Of these the first two will most likely apply to someone setting out as a sole trader or on the bottom rung of the SME (small to medium enterprise) ladder. The third may involve more investment and the last two may require serious third party funding.

Our first example is Alice, an experienced public relations manager in a national PR agency, based at a high profile city in the South of England commanding national attention with a strong base in science, technology, manufacturing and education, who decided to go local on her own. Let's call this

Case A. The essence of Alice's concept was to give a more human, hands on service to local enterprises at a significantly lower cost than a nationally branded agency. The concept relies on satisfying the second and third criteria.

The second example (Case B) is also a local business addressing all of the first three USP factors. Fred is a qualified plumber, already self-employed, who works freelance for a number of private sector building contractors and developers on new housing projects within his local area. The rates of pay that he can earn as a subcontractor are a fraction of the main contractors' charges to local authorities and developers. He is also a dab hand at painting and decorating and as a glazier. Fred thinks he can do better serving owners of older homes who have regular and occasional demands for repairs, renovation and maintenance of their properties. His concept is grounded on friendly, quality service at lower charges than local firms who have grown into substantial businesses on the back of lucrative new housing and office developments and who factor overhead costs and management charges into their quotations.

Case C involves technical innovation. Simon is a skilled software systems engineer working for a large international managed services provider. He has achieved a middle management position and travels widely but his career prospects are limited and he would like to spend more time with his young family. Recently, the fuel oil tank in Simon's garden was raided during the night and drained of more than £1,000 of fuel for which he was uninsured.

He perceives fuel theft as a major risk for householders, schools and village halls in rural neighbourhoods throughout the UK and has designed an app which can be connected to a locked fuel tank cap and can be activated remotely by those with the entry code. This solves the problem of manually locked caps which need to be unlocked any time that the oil supplier delivers and the householders may be absent. Simon has found a British manufacturer of manually locked caps who is interested in his technology. Alternatively, Simon has identified a manufacturer of remote controlled caps in Australia and could negotiate a distribution agreement.

Cases A and B are real and Case C is imaginary, but Case D, which conceived a global opportunity in intellectual property (IP), is a project which I pursued some four years ago. The concept was to create an online marketplace for brand and trademark license trading and transactions. Based on membership subscriptions, the digital platform would connect brand owners and their agents seeking to sell IP licenses to other manufacturers or service providers looking for high recognition brands, trademarks or designs to adopt. Commission would be charged on completed transactions and collected online together with licensing fees. Unlike the three previous cases, Case D required substantial up front funding for sophisticated new software and website development before the product could be offered to potential users.

All four concepts make sense and seem attractive but much work needs to be done to verify whether there are practical market opportunities. Your concept will also require similar research, however self-evident its merits may seem to you.

BASIC RESEARCH TO DEFINE YOUR MARKET

There are two research strands in defining your market: quantifying the value and charting the channels to market.

Quantifying value
There may be some difficulty in establishing an absolute value for your service or product. And the numbers you come up with may not be wholly meaningful.

The limitations of what is possible are illustrated in terms of the four concept cases outlined above:

Case A

Alice used an online survey which she sent digitally to all businesses and other organisations in her catchment area having an annual sales value of £100,000, the minimum she felt would be able to support basic HR consultancy. She analysed the results into four sectors: manufacturing industry, business services, science and technology establishments and local government/public services plus charities. She found that the strongest sectors in terms of current or potential HR spend were manufacturing, business services and a handful of charities. Assuming an average spend of £5,000 the realistic target market value was assessed at £1,250,000 – just sufficient to justify her start-up. Alice's initial survey was supplemented by 50 telephone and face to face interviews with established contacts within each sector.

Case B

Fred's research was rather less structured. He knew that there were 1,500,000 older homes in what he regarded as his catchment area and from observation driving around the villages he could see that many properties were more than 100 years old with some of them being listed buildings. He estimated that on average these homeowners would replace or improve either their bathrooms, showers or kitchens at least once every 10 years and with installation work of no less than £500 a job (excluding hardware), the minimum market value for his services would be £75,000 per annum plus call-outs for maintenance work and emergencies. He supported this calculation by consulting with friendly contacts in other building trades: electrical and heating engineers. For Fred this seemed a reasonable market to attack and he realised then that if he was successful he would have to take on additional staff or an apprentice.

Case C

Valuing the market for Simon's remote control fuel cap lock was more difficult.

The UK manufacturer of mechanical fuel caps was able to tell him how many they sold nationally and he postulated a premium selling price, including delivery, of £65 against £52 for the standard product. However, quantifying how many would convert to the remote control product or how many unsecured fuel tank owners might be tempted to buy the sophisticated new product was no better than guesswork. In the end, Simon came up with a minimum potential market of 60,000 units over three years and a maximum of 500,000 units.

Case D

We started with global statistics of IP activity. Every year 7 million new trademarks and brands are registered. We found that in 2013 royalty revenues of $5.6 billion were generated from the licensing of trademarks and brands in the top 5 product sectors in the US and Canada alone. Of course, these mouth-watering statistics were virtually meaningless in helping us to frame realistic projections, except to say that the potential market for our concept was vast. In the end, what we did was to take conservative targets for a build-up in revenue from membership subscriptions of £1,000 and scalable commission at a basic rate of 15% on completed transactions from the second year onwards. This enabled us to forecast revenue rising from £30,000 in the first year to £600,000 in the third.

Whatever the limitations, you must carry out the quantification exercise at this early stage. It is the first test of whether your concept is realistic and a primary ingredient for business planning.

Channels to market

Having identified a value for your market you need to check its credibility by deciding how you are going to penetrate it in order to generate sales. This is commonly described as defining the "channels to market".

The internet and social media are powerful, cheap tools for

communicating with potential customers but for businesses focused solely on the area in which they are located the traditional tools may be more effective. Local newspaper advertising and editorial in print or online, leaflet drops and telephone cold calling all have their place. For service businesses (Alice in Case A and Fred in Case B) the best way to get your business off the ground with its first paying customers may be networking. Do not hesitate to call up people for whom you have completed work to their satisfaction in your previous employment – if they have no requirement they may provide referrals to others that arc looking for a supplier.

In Alice's case, she had no service contract with her previous employer to restrict her from soliciting their PR clients and was able to approach openly people who had enjoyed working with her but were less happy with the company.

For Fred, a fruitful channel to market was the network of qualified tradesmen, especially heating engineers and electricians with whom he had worked previously as sub-contractors on building projects and who had their own private homeowner clientele. In fact, as his business moved up to larger assignments, such as complete kitchen refits, he would be able to put together project teams from these sources on the basis of their reciprocal collaboration. Fred also decided to take repeat advertising in a popular local freesheet which listed selected maintenance and repair services for the homeowner and placed small advertisements on the websites of selected village halls and parish councils.

The freesheet advertising was successful but his first and only excursion into digital marketing yielded little.

Simon's effective channels to market for his Case C remote control fuel cap were more diverse. His first resource was the databank of the traditional security fuel cap manufacturer with whom he decided to work and its catalogue and website. But he needed to spread the net wider. With perseverance he was able to attract editorial in some trade magazines which helped gain attention. Another important route to the consumer was through local fuel oil distributors and the managers of regional fuel oil distribution schemes, although that involved paying commission which reduced his profit margins. So far, Simon is addressing the UK market only but his medium term intention is to export into other European countries. He has no plans how to do this yet.

Our Case D project, by definition, demanded global marketing from the outset based on a sophisticated online platform and enabling members to source IP trading opportunities, digitally negotiate and complete transactions. We needed to build databases of prominent brand and trademark owners from key industries, IP merchandisers and registered agents, representing the supply side of the market, and of manufacturers and service providers from other selected industries, the demand side, who were potential IP purchasers and licensees. Having established the databases, we would market to them by mass email campaigns. To start we would send emails to selected major brand and trademark owners who handled their licensing in-house and leading IP merchandisers. We were able to conduct preliminary trade research with both categories of player at the 2015 Brand Licensing Europe Show at Olympia. The main obstacles were the time and cost involved in creating the complex online platform.

When you have clearly defined the channels to market for your concept against a target market value, you now have a basic business proposition on which you can take soundings and test reactions from objective third parties.

ASK A FRIEND

So far, when designing and putting some flesh on the skeleton of your concept, you have been carried forward by your enthusiasm, possibly with encouragement from your partner at home. The next stage in your journey will be detailed planning which is more rigorous and will apply stress-testing to the basic concept. Before committing the considerable time and effort required to this process, you will find it useful to discuss your embryonic enterprise with business people who are more objective and whose opinions you respect.

It is less likely that there is some fatal flaw in your thinking (although that is always possible) but more likely that there are some aspects of your product or service and its delivery to which you have not paid sufficient attention and which could ruin your enterprise if not corrected. In fact, I would say that "Ask a friend" or, preferably several friends, is an essential step in the preliminaries which you would ignore at your own risk.

Whom should I consult?
The optimum is someone who knows you well enough in a business connection to judge your capabilities and who has started up their own business with some success. You may not find anyone who fits that profile completely and, therefore, more than one assessor is advisable. Someone who knows the field of business in which you intend to work may add valuable comment. Perhaps a person who has tried to launch a business in a similar market to yours and failed or achieved only modified success. If your product or service is innovative, try to consult a player or service provider in the relevant industry. Take careful note of what they say both before and after you try to convince them of the merits of your concept.

Typical comments
Don't expect to receive unqualified encouragement; that is not what you are after. Sensible reservations against a generally favourable cautionary comments will be helpful. Outright dismissal of your concept would, of course, be a serious deterrent. The following are some of the more common negative opinions which may be voiced:

- *You are entering a very competitive field (your USP may not be strong enough to gain entry.)*
- *You'll probably get there in the end but it will take longer than you expect.*
- *The idea's great and you have the skills to deliver, but I wonder if you have the experience and sales ability to secure business.*
- *The product is innovative but your customers may be happy with what they have available now.*
- *You're asking people to change the way they conduct their business and the market may not be ready for it yet.*
- *You will have difficulty in attracting the funding you need to develop and carry out your project.*
- *Having always worked in a team of people, you'll find it difficult to work alone.*
- *After years of regular salary you need to be sure that you (and your family) can adjust to having no secure income.*

Some of these points shed doubt on your concept and its market acceptance; others suggest that the start-up period will be longer than you had expected; the last two question your ability to make a go of it or manage the stress involved in transferring from a more secure environment. If these are the reservations you encounter, it will be a matter of personal judgment as to how many negatives would cause you to abandon the project. The last two points are questions that you have already considered; you may want to think them through again.

Unless you encounter a barrage of negative comments, it is unlikely that you will decide to abandon the project. It is more likely that you will go back to the drawing board to refine the concept or its channels to market. You will certainly want to factor in to the business planning process that comes next any adjustments you may make to your previous definitions. You may also consider it wise to develop a Plan B in the event that the project lacks traction or fails completely. Either way, as William Shakespeare put it more eloquently than I could articulate:

"And thus the native hue of resolution
Is sicklied o'er with the pale cast of thought..."

— *Polonius, Hamlet, William Shakespeare, 1564-1616*

2

PLANNING

"The best laid schemes of mice and men
Gang oft a'glay"

– Robert Burns (1759-1796)

I doubt that Rabbie Burns was thinking of business plans when he wrote of 'schemes' in the 18th century, but the cap fits. Few business plans survive events without amendment and plans for start-ups always need regular revision. But that is not an argument for not planning. In this chapter I will try to define the planning that you should do in order to provide a working plan for your new business as you start up.

HOW MUCH AND FOR HOW LONG

The business plans that you need for third party consumption when seeking finance are of a different order and I will return to the subject of planning for this purpose in Chapter 4. The focus for now is on what you need and what will help you most. And my first piece of advice is to adopt as your watchword the well-known acronym **KISS: Keep it Simple, Stupid.**

In light of that stricture, let's begin by considering the form that your plan should take and the period of time that it should cover. At this stage, cashflow is more important than net profit and the key elements of your plan will be:

- Sales revenue
- Direct or variable costs, % related proportionally to sales, such as commission and required materials
- Gross profit (sales revenue less direct costs)
- Office and general equipment costs for the running of the business
- Salaries (if any)
- Travel and motoring expenses
- Net operating profit

Before discussing each element in turn, we need to decide what planning period is most useful for your purposes. There used to be a perception that all serious business planning required a detailed five-year plan. We'll consider the demands of external investors in Chapter 4, but for start-up entrepreneurs anything more than two years at this stage is a waste of time. Projections beyond two years fall into the category of conjecture and are probably no more than wishful thinking. Therefore, my second piece of advice is to forget five-year planning for now.

However, you should certainly plan month by month for the first year and probably for the second year also. A good reason for constructing your plan on income received (classified by accountants as revenue), and planned payments (expenditure) is that it will double as your Budget. For the first, but far from the last time, in this book I emphasize that cashflow is much more important to all start-ups than net profit.

Monthly projections at the outset enable you to monitor progress not just by variances from plan/budget but also by substituting month-end "actuals" for forecast numbers and then revising and rolling forward your monthly forecasts into the next 12 months ahead as a reiterative monthly process.

Another good reason for two year rolling plans is that you may have in mind step changes in sales revenue or costs which, if not game changers, will have a significant impact on cashflow and profitability. Returning to the start-up example of Case A in Chapter 1, Alice may have in mind adding an account manager in the second year to supplement her front line role in her PR business or moving her office from the spare bedroom at home into rented business premises. The timing of either action will depend on progress and will have a significant impact on monthly cashflow. Therefore, her planning should allow for flexibility in monthly forecasts.

SENSIBLE SALES TARGETS

This first line of your business plan is the most challenging. The scoping exercises of Chapter One may have set the parameters for sales targets that are feasible but have barely addressed how long it will take to reach a viable level of business. You should always take a conservative view of the necessary build up period. There are three points to be made here:

1. Unless you have firm customers or contracts before you start, be prepared to wait 3-6 months before the cash starts to roll in (probably longer for Simon's Case C's new product and much longer for our Case D's IP service.)

2. Beware of what I call the 'feast or famine' syndrome. This problem occurs when you finally gain contracts and are fully occupied in delivering your services to satisfy current demands so that you have no time to develop new ones. If you allow this to happen, when

current work assignments are completed you fall into famine without income until you have negotiated new work. What's more, you have lost momentum and have to re-start your sales campaign. A business that operates in fits and starts will inevitably fail to gain traction in the marketplace and very likely fail.

Your remedy is always to set aside a proportion of your time, perhaps as much as one day a week, whatever the workload, to concentrate on developing new and repeat customers, thereby increasing your sales pipeline. Remember that the most valuable commodity in your business is your time and to act accordingly (if one day a week seems too much, take into account that you will probably be initially working no less than six).

3. Related to the feast or famine phenomenon is the situation of managers who have been taken or been 'given' early retirement and are awarded a limited period contract to provide services as a self-employed subcontractor or consultant. This may give you the confidence to 'go solo' but don't be deceived by any false sense of security. Unless you go through the routine of Chapter 1 processes, you won't know whether the services you are providing for your former employer will find a competitive niche in the marketplace and whether you can price them at the same level as your contract (don't delay too long before finding out).

As an example, take the case of Mark, the son of a friend, who is an expert IT systems designer and accepted a one year contract to provide the same services on projects for the well-known company that had employed him for some years and was now seeking to replace its fixed staff costs by variable cost consultancy. The first year was fine and his lifestyle and standard of living were unaffected. Towards the end of the year he started to look for alternative consultancy work elsewhere and found, to his surprise, that there was no demand for his services at the same price. Fortunately, he was able to negotiate a six month extension of his existing contract while he set about repackaging his service offer as a lower priced consultancy and reducing his cost base.

PRICING PARAMETERS

Pricing strategy has two determinants: the price that the market will bear, and the need to cover your costs with a margin for profit. We can consider the first element now because it helps establish both the upper and lower limits for your pricing and also the maximum revenue you can generate from the capacity you have to deliver your products or services. The second element can be addressed only after you have calculated your cost base and we will calculate shortly the minimum prices you require to cover your costs in the context of profit projections. There are risks in both under-pricing and over-pricing, but it is generally easier to start higher and then lower your prices, rather than starting lower and attempting to introduce higher prices in the short and medium-term.

MARKET PRICING

Customer purchasing decisions are taken on perceived value for money and cost comparisons. I say 'perceived' value because clever marketing, branding, packaging and advertising can distort brand preference and add value to competing products. Therefore, you need to take the following factors into account:

- If you are marketing your business on quality rather than price, low pricing may send out the wrong message.
- As a start-up business, if you don't know what your price should be it is easier to start higher and then lower your price later.
- Make sure that you have fully costed all your product or service inputs before finalizing your prices.

For our four cases, the thought processes are dissimilar. For Cases A and B, both Alice and Fred are aiming to offer high quality service at a lower cost than larger competitors. For Case C, Simon already has a fixed number from his research on the unit price for his remote control fuel tank cap that the market will bear. In Case D we were flying blind and were guided in setting the membership cost for our IP trading platform by the rates of annual fees which the leading trade association charged their members.

A major constraint on both Alice's and Fred's businesses is their available time. For Alice's PR agency there is a limit on the number of customers she can handle personally and client meetings that she can attend. However, she knows that she can maximize the use of her time by delegating back office functions (e.g. designing press releases, booking editorial in the media, collecting press clippings and other data, work on clients' website content and researching publicity opportunities) to part-time staff. Treating this and any other sub-contracting as a variable job cost, Alice knows that her charges have to cover this and generate a sufficient margin on planned sales (her gross profit) to cover all fixed costs. As well as office overheads and travel costs, her fixed costs will include basic monthly payments to herself. One mitigating factor is that she may be able to agree retainer arrangements with clients that will cover a minimum fixed amount of her consultancy work, which are acceptable within clients' annual budgets and provide for additional charges for further work commissioned. This will also underpin cashflow, which is a significant advantage for any start-up business.

Fred in Case B does not enjoy the advantage of customer retainers and can't venture into the territory of annual boiler maintenance contracts with payment by instalments because he is not a qualified heating engineer. But he can offer an immediate cost saving to the private households that are his customer base by not registering for VAT until his sales approach the HMRC entry level for compulsory registration (see Chapter 6). This gives him a 20% price advantage initially over any larger firm competition.

COST PRICING

Fred's one man plumbing business provides a good illustration of how to price according to cost. He has no variable costs other than equipment or replacement components, which he procures and purchases for the customer. He charges them out at cost, but he may choose to retain the benefit of any trade discount when he is making the purchase.

In pricing his time and labour he is conscious of his motoring costs in making customer visits and therefore includes a fixed call out charge for most jobs based on the weekly cost divided by the expected number of calls which includes the first hour of his time in attendance. Since the distances from his home base to the first visit and between visits during the day is variable, he will be out of pocket some days and make a profit on other days from the call out charge. Otherwise, Fred prices his labour according to the time spent on site at each visit over and above the first hour.

In his simple business plan, Fred expects to make an average of 3 calls a day for 5 days a week and factors in a call out charge of £50 with a second hour at £35. His business plan is therefore based on an average weekly gross income of £1,275 as summarised below:

	per day	per week
	£	£
Sales	255	1,275

If his operating costs including motor expenses and the overheads of his office at home, which his wife operates as an employee, are £655 a week, his weekly net income will be £620 giving him £2,440 in a four week month before tax.

This modestly successful outcome will be enhanced in a 31 day month with an extra two days gross income of £510 or, if he increases his jobs per day from 3 to 4, his monthly net income would be raised by £1700 less some increase in motor expenses.

The other cases are more complicated but all depend on getting the price and sales volume projections right. Case C, where Simon's gross margins will be tight after direct costs, is volume driven and the speed at which sales grow will be critical in developing sufficient gross profit to cover overheads. Likewise, for Case D our challenge was to generate sufficient income from membership fees to cover all operating costs until such time as commission on completed IP transactions started up in the second year – and that was based on the assumption that shareholder investment would provide for all development expenditure (in particular the development of the digital platform).

Case A is more akin to Case B, with first year back office staffing treated as a variable cost, but otherwise the need to cover motoring and minimal establishment costs before Alice can pay herself is paramount.

MANAGING ON A SHOESTRING

If you are coming from a corporate culture, there will be many facilities that you may take for granted as essential to your working environment. While you are planning to start up your business, this is the moment to question them all and to whittle them down to those that you really need for the opening months and very likely longer.

Let's start with a checklist to define what you must have and what you may **not** need to run your business efficiently:

Office and communications equipment
- An office – Can you manage working from home? What you must have is a space where you can work undisturbed and concentrate without distractions. If you have a family you may need to establish 'house rules' including periods when your working space is out of bounds to all.

- A second telephone line for the business. Possibly not initially, if all members of the household are drilled to answer calls with a business identity during office working hours. Alternatively, a mobile number could be your second business number. An answer machine is essential to take messages in your absence.

- A computer or laptop with decent capacity is essential for email correspondence, raising invoices and maintaining a database. A strong and uninterrupted internet connection is obviously essential.

- A printer is the third piece of essential home office equipment. Be sure to buy one that has a built-in scanning capability as increasingly signed documents are transmitted online through scanning and email.

Travel by public transport
- Travel is probably an inevitable part of your business. If you have to attend meetings in a large city from well outside, forget any idea of travelling by car. You may be able to kid yourself that the out of pocket

expense is less than by rail, but you will be losing out on work time which could be spent on emails, calls to customers or office administration when travelling by train. And if you can travel at off-peak times into and from the main cities, you are likely to make substantial savings on rail fares.

Motoring expenses

- Motoring on business other than driving to the station is unavoidable for those operating local businesses, certainly for Alice and Fred in Cases A and B although their circumstances differ. Until she establishes a separate office outside her home all of Alice's meetings will be at her clients' offices or other premises. She will need a car that is reliable, cheap to run and modest (these days nobody is impressed by flashy new vehicles suggesting that they have been paid for from clients' fees). If she uses her car for private travel as well as business she will still be able to claim an appropriate proportion of the total cost as an allowable expense for tax purposes (see more in Chapter 6).

- Fred's situation is clear-cut. Unless he has a garage at home or lock-up nearby, his vehicle will double as transport, equipment and parts store and also mobile office, if he manages his appointments on the move and even raises and sends his invoices after calls by mobile. Therefore, he needs a sturdy van. If his business name or logo is printed on the sides he will establish it as a business vehicle and have little difficulty in establishing all running expenses as tax allowable.

- Financing a car or van for business use is much the same as for a private use vehicle with a range of lease and hire purchase alternatives. Although two or three year leasing deals may have attractive terms enabling the acquisition of a superior vehicle, they carry substantial risk. In the event that the business fails and you can no longer afford the monthly charge, there will probably be a hefty penalty for terminating the lease. The cheapest and least risky way to fund outright purchase is a bank loan which can be repaid by selling the vehicle, as can an outstanding hire purchase (HP) debt.

Business entertaining
- Maybe you come from a work environment where buying lunch for clients or associates or even gifts at Christmas is considered customary in building relationships. Happily, business entertaining has tapered off over recent years, even in larger companies, and any suggestion that a supplier contract award has been influenced by hospitality received may fall foul of corporate governance standards. Therefore, you should shun business entertaining when starting up your business as an avoidable expense.
- The same goes for accepting hospitality from those to whom you are trying to sell your services for a similar reason. Those entertaining you may think, however misguidedly, that it entitles them to preferential terms.
- There are exceptions to these rules in the case of suppliers who have travelled from abroad to meet you or current and prospective clients whom you visit at your own expense. Neither situation is likely as you start up your business. Of our examples, only Case C might qualify as Simon tries to develop distributorships internationally. Otherwise, meeting over a cup of coffee will suffice.

Book-keeping and accountancy
- For the first year you should try to manage all book-keeping yourself. The number of transactions will be

limited and maintaining basic records should not be too burdensome. (More on this subject in Chapter 5.)

- Provided that you are capable of handling your own tax returns without assistance you will not need the services of a qualified accountant until your business is incorporated as a limited company or partnership, in which case annual returns will need to be filed, even if, assuming you are initially under the threshold, Abbreviated Accounts will be accepted by HMRC.

PROFIT AND CASHFLOW PROJECTIONS

By now you should have considered most of the elements of your business plan including some that we have not discussed such as vehicle and premises insurance, office heating, electricity, water and council tax. While your home remains your office, you could include a reasonable proportion of your premises costs, say 20%, among your business overheads in the profit and loss account but not in personal cashflow projections because you are going to incur the outlay on those domestic charges anyway and pay them from your household budget. It is a moot point whether or not to include such overhead costs in your profit projections. My advice is against, unless you plan to have a partner or shareholders in your business from the outset, in which case you will want to establish your right to make these charges.

Profit projections
The sales data will be based on your forecasts of invoices month by month and theoretically all expenses by the timing of your expected dates of supplier invoicing. However, it makes sense to treat periodic bills such as those for utilities and telephone as monthly charges which better reflect ongoing usage. For third parties viewing your projections,

this approach presents a more even picture for the progression of the business.

As discussed at the beginning of this chapter, the principal lines of your business plan will be sales, gross profit and net operating income, with intermediate lines for items of direct cost, indirect cost and their totals. By adding a further line for cumulative net operating profit the month-by-month format will show when the business moves from loss to profit.

You can also calculate your break-even point quite simply to show what level of monthly sales you need to achieve equilibrium. If the gross contribution to overheads (your gross profit) is, say, X per cent of sales, and your fixed costs are Y then the sales required are :

$$\frac{Y}{X}$$

In Alice's case, as an example, if her PR business's monthly overheads are initially £2,500 and she costs her contracts so that variable costs are projected at 20% of invoiced sales, her contribution to overheads is 80% and it follows that she breaks even at a monthly sales level of £3,125. Sadly, business life is rarely that simple. Gross profit margins are usually not uniform with the proportion of actual direct costs varying between jobs, products and customers. However, it is useful to keep a simplified idea of minimum sales at the forefront of your mind.

Cashflow projections
We come now to the most important part of your planning for practical purposes. Calculating and updating your cashflow regularly is probably something you have been doing for years with your bank statements as a "back of the envelope" exercise. Now you need to construct a more formal framework for doing the same with your business on a longer term basis. The starting point is the profit projection that you have just made, unless you prefer to construct your cashflow projections first and then work backwards to a profits forecast.

To convert your profit projections to a cashflow forecast, adjust your sales to revenue by substituting month of receipt for month of invoice and expenses to expenditure by substituting month of planned payment for month charged. Your two bottom lines now become net cashflow and cumulative net cashflow which tell you exactly what you expect the bank account of the business to show at the end of each month.

The net effect of these adjustments, unless you are running a cash only business, is likely to be negative, particularly in the opening year of any new business, because the time lags between billing and payment don't work in your favour.

The invoices you issue will typically be paid by customers no sooner than the next month on 30-day terms, whereas some of your expenses, such as telephone bills, require prompter payment and others are paid by monthly direct debit at fixed dates. These calculations will help you to analyse what working capital you need to get started and the level of bank overdraft you may be seeking.

As previously noted, cashflow projecting is an ongoing reiterative exercise best carried out monthly. With the rolling cashflow process that I recommend, which looks forward 12 months, the exercise consists of substituting actual receipts and payments at the month end for the amounts forecast, revisiting and revising the onward forecasts if necessary after carrying forward the actual cumulative balance. This helps to avoid unpleasant shocks and reduces the incidence of sleepless nights.

FURTHER EVALUATION

You've finished your basic business planning but there is time for further reflection and reassessment before you spring into action. There are three final exercises to be taken: a SWOT analysis, stress testing and third-party assessment.

SWOT analysis

Originating from the 1960s and 1970s as a tool for strategic planning, the concept is sometimes attributed to Albert Humphrey, who led group conventions at the Stanford Research Institute (now SRI International) using data from the Fortune 500 companies. I first encountered SWOT during management training at the US multinational I was then working for in 1980. You might consider it to sound a little 'old hat' but SWOT analysis has stood the test of time and is still very much in use.

Often displayed as a 2x2 matrix, there are four elements in a SWOT analysis:

- Strengths: characteristics of the business (or project) that give it an advantage over others
- Weaknesses: characteristics of the business that place it at a disadvantage relative to others
- Opportunities: elements in the environment that the business could exploit to its advantage
- Threats: elements in the environment that could cause trouble for the business

Applying SWOT to your start-up may seem like using a sledgehammer to crack a nut but it is not pretentious. You will be surprised how thought provoking it can be. You have already addressed Opportunities and Threats in your Chapter 1 research to define the market. Now, you can bring your planning experience to bear in appraising your venture's Strengths and Weaknesses.

Stress Testing

How robust are your profit projections and how vulnerable to unplanned shortfalls in sales or increases in cost? At the least, your business should be sufficiently strong to survive a 10% reduction in sales, increases of 10% in any cost element or of 5% in total overheads.

Some investors apply more stringent criteria. One consultancy client of mine, on the hunt for private businesses in which he could both invest and take an active part, used a 30% reduction in sales and any consequent cost reductions that might be made as his stress test. Not surprisingly, he never made an investment while I was advising him.

Third party assessment
Armed with your Business Plan, a brief summary of your game plan and assumptions for the profit projections plus your SWOT analysis, you can now go back to the people with whom you consulted previously on your business concept and who reacted positively. There is no need to include your cashflow projections in this package, which remain a personal forecast until you start your search for funding. Potential investors will certainly want to view cashflow projections and I'll advise you how best to present them in Chapter 4.

Your objective, as before, is to garner constructive criticism but you should also take into account any negative comments received. It will also be useful to go back to some of those who gave the original concept a thumbs down. If any now modify or even change their opinions that will provide real encouragement. Be sure to include in the consultation process this time at least one businessperson who has started a similar business successfully or someone who has tried and failed.

Third party assessment may cause you to adjust the detail of your business plan or the timescale for getting it off the ground, in which case make the adjustments and evaluate yourself again.

Decision time
Having assessed the body of evidence before you, your own evaluation together with the assessments of others, this is the time when you have to decide whether or not to go forward into choosing the structure of your business and searching actively for any necessary third party finance to launch the enterprise. Inevitably the final decision will be subjective.

If you conclude that the risks outweigh the opportunities, you are faced with two alternatives:

- Either go back to the drawing board, modify your concept drastically or come up with a new one and go through the planning process again; *or*
- Abandon your intention of striking out on your own and make the best of what you are doing now.

There is no disgrace in jumping ship before the boat sails. The mistake would be to soldier on (mixing my military metaphors here) without full confidence that you can succeed. That way failure is almost assured.

I close this chapter by reminding you of a familiar literary figure who was no business planner but certainly had an eye for cash management:

"Annual income twenty pounds, annual expenditure nineteen nineteen six – result happiness. Annual income twenty pounds, annual expenditure – twenty pounds ought and sixpence, result misery."

– Mr. Micawber, David Copperfield, Charles Dickens (1812-1870)

3

STRUCTURING YOUR BUSINESS

"When we mean to build,
We first survey the plot, then draw the model;
And when we see the figure of the house,
Then must we rate the cost of the erection."

– Henry IV, Part 2, William Shakespeare (1564-1616)

So far, you have developed and refined the concept for your business and, in the last chapter, written a basic plan which you believe to be viable. It's time now to get down to the practical detail of structuring your business so that you can manage it yourself in its early stages without external input and in compliance with the requirements of company law. It is also important that the structure of your business is clearly defined and transparent to any third-party searches from those seeking to do business with you. A clearly defined structure is a prerequisite for any private investor or financial institution whom you approach to provide funds.

REGISTRATION OF BUSINESS NAME

Whether or not you mean to start the business as a sole trader or a limited company, you need to establish an identity by registering a business name. Registration is simple via various low-cost online solutions. Each of them will enable you to search the business name you wish to register having checked first whether or not it is already in use. The majority will then register your business and file default or uploaded bespoke paperwork with Companies House as well as providing a Certificate of Registration for a fee of under £50. They will usually try to upsell other services such as share certificates, business packs and email and website packages; so think carefully about the essentials that you require at the point of company registration.

Your selection of business name is a personal choice but you might like to bear the following in mind:

- There's merit in including your actual name in the business title if you want to give an impression of friendly personal service. However, anonymity may be preferable if your business is not entirely local or as a protection in the event of financial difficulty later on. Of the four examples that we featured in Chapter 1, Cases A and B are both personalised services and could benefit from the inclusion of their owners' names in the business title; Cases C and D would not.

- Acronyms or fake brand names such as "Acme Boilers" are tempting but have become debased by the multitude of online entries in every field of commercial activity displayed on the internet. "Acme Services" is wholly uninformative.

- Including an indication of the service or product provided is useful but requires careful consideration, particularly if you later pivot or diversify the business.

- However, "beauty is in the eye of the beholder" and, as I said, the choice is entirely yours from the wise to the whimsical, from the mundane to the striking.

SOLE TRADER VS LIMITED COMPANY

There are advantages and disadvantages in starting your business as a sole trader or a limited company, such as those below, so you should weigh up carefully before taking a decision.

Risk
A limited company provides its shareholders, directors and management with protection against creditors, claims and legal action, provided that those authorised to make commitments on behalf of the company make it clear that they are not acting in a personal capacity. Company information should be included on all orders, invoices and agreements.

A sole trader has no such protection and, in the event of business failure or claims from third parties, the owner's assets are at risk without limit. In some cases the risks can be mitigated by taking out professional insurance, but premiums are expensive.

Nevertheless, the owners and directors of limited companies are not entirely invulnerable. When setting up a bank overdraft or loan for a new company its directors are often required to provide personal guarantees against default and repayment within the terms of the lender's agreement. In the case of larger sums invested by institutions or private equity, controlling shareholders who are not directors may be called upon to guarantee any loan element in the funding package. There will be more on this subject in Chapter 4.

Under the Companies Act, directors who misuse their positions or company funds and commit acts of fraud or malfeasance (a legal term for corporate wrong-doing) are held liable and may be subject to criminal charges. On the other hand, a sole trader is under no constraint, other than their own good sense, not to take money from his business because they are in any case personally liable to their creditors without qualification.

However, a registered sole trader is constrained by

definition from taking in a partner or shareholder and if they wish to do that they will have to restructure their business.

Administration
When starting your business you will want to conserve your time by keeping unproductive administration to a minimum. Sole traders are at an advantage in the following respects:

- They do not have to keep formal books of account. Until they develop a multitude of clients and suppliers they can probably run the business through a simple cashbook in which they enter all cash received, invoices paid and charges against their bank account by direct debit, standing order, and debit card. Supported by a diary that logs appointments, they can file invoices raised and received in date order in separate files and may not even choose to maintain daybooks. (See Chapter 5 for more on small business accounting).

- They do not pay themselves a salary and will not have to maintain PAYE records until they employ staff.

- No VAT records until the sole trader registers for VAT (See Chapter 6).

- No formal annual accounts required for filing although they will need to construct a trading account and capital allowances schedule when preparing to file their annual self-employed income tax return.

- Flexibility. If they decide at any time in the future to incorporate their business as a limited company, the transition is relatively painless.

As a sole trader you will need to inform the income tax and social security authorities that you will be self-employed.

Also, if you have any doubts about the approved use of your property for business purposes you would be wise to consult the local planning officer. Unless you are employing staff on site, there should be no objections.

Remember that if your business has a name other than your own, you must put your own name on your letterhead and invoices. A suitable format would be:

Fred Bloggs
trading as
FB Home Maintenance Services
[Address]
[Telephone Number]
[Email address]
[Website – optional]

In contrast, starting up as a limited company involves formal registration and the filing of an opening return detailing the shareholders and officers of the company followed by the regular annual return and a raft of documentation described below. You can hire an accountant to carry out all of this for you but, as we noted in the previous chapter, that is an expense that can be deferred until later. Filing a company's opening registration at Companies House is not particularly onerous and you can do it on line in less than an hour when you have assembled all the data. As above, many online services will file all of the initial required paperwork as part of their service.

Banking
As a sole trader you could run your business banking through your personal current account but that is inappropriate if it is a joint account with your domestic partner. In any case, it will be easier to manage the records of your business transactions if you open a separate account at your bank. With the evidence of your registration certificate opening the new account should be straightforward.

PARTNERSHIPS AND PEOPLE

It may be that you have one or more valued friend(s) or colleague(s) with whom you want to set up your business. Before considering the suitability of partners and their selection you need to be aware of the alternative forms of partnership that are available.

In a partnership each member makes a contribution to the business: skills, property (real estate or IP), money, ideas or some combination of these. Each partner's responsibilities and rights will be defined in a partnership agreement and management participation and profit share will vary according to the form of partnership chosen. There are three alternative forms:

- General Partnership
- Limited Partnership
- Limited Liability Partnership (LLP)

Whichever form of partnership you choose, it is important that there should be a formal agreement in writing before you start. If you want to go 50-50 in all decision making and share all assets, liabilities and profit distributions, it is no good just saying so and putting both your names on a letterhead and other business stationery. You will have little idea at the outset how well the business will progress or whether the relationship will stand the test of time. As one Ian Fleming opines, "Nothing propinks like propinquity" and at some time in the future one or other of you may want to pull out of the partnership when a clearly written and signed agreement will help greatly to avoid any dispute.

General partnership
General partners share equal rights and responsibilities in managing the business. Under the UK Partnership Act 1890 each partner has joint and several liability and any individual

partner can bind the entire partnership to a legal obligation. Personal liability for all of the business's debts and obligations presents additional risks to those of the sole trader, who is liable only for his own mistakes and misjudgements, and emphasises that you will need a high degree of confidence in any partner whom you take in.

However, there is a significant tax advantage to a partnership that we will refer to again in Chapter 5: partnership profits are not taxed to the business but pass through to the partners, who include the income they received in their individual annual tax returns.

Limited partnership

Under a limited partnership one partner must have general partnership status with exposure to full personal liability as above but the other partners can restrict their personal liability to the amount of their investment in the business.

Under this arrangement, the general partner retains the right to control the business while the limited partner(s) take no part in management decision-making. This provides the general partner with some degree of protection, but you will still want to think carefully before accepting either role.

Limited Liability Partnership (LLP)

LLPs in the UK are governed by the twin Limited Liability Partnership Acts in Great Britain (2000) and Northern Ireland (2002) with regulation consolidated in the Companies Act 2006. LLP members have joint responsibility to the extent that they may define it in an LLP Agreement but individuals do not carry responsibility for each other's actions. As with shareholders in a limited company, LLP members cannot lose more than they invest except in the event of fraud, wrongdoing or personal guarantees.

The LLP is highly flexible and was originally lobbied for by the Big Four accountancy firms seeking to limit liability for their audits. Since 2003 it has been adopted by many law and accountancy firms, both big and small. An existing partnership that wishes to convert to LLP status can simply file an application for registration and has no need to modify its existing partnership agreement. In the UK the Inland Revenue treats LLPs as tax-transparent like other forms of partnership with income or gains distributed gross to partners as self-employed persons, rather than PAYE employees.

Partner selection

Choosing a partner is a sensitive exercise in human relations which is best conducted with complete candour by both parties. Neither of you will wish to repent at leisure; so take your time and discuss every aspect of how you would work together. For example, if you are starting a service business, it will be important that you have the same attitude to customer relations and service standards.

Be sure that you are satisfied with what each of you brings to the partnership and with the division of responsibilities. In a small business it is generally better that you have complementary skills and experience rather supplementing each other's within the same environment. Personal chemistry is important but be wary of duplicating each other's weaknesses as well as strengths and this applies particularly to risk-taking.

Good friends who have worked together for many years in the same industry or even company as colleagues are particularly vulnerable. If you both decide to seek pastures new at the same time because you are dissatisfied with your careers and have the opportunity to take early retirement, it is all too easy to believe that you will be stronger together in shared self-employment. As an analogy, the mental picture of two sailors who can't swim being cast overboard and clutching each other to drown together is not inappropriate.

However, there is some comfort in knowing that if the partnership does not prosper it is easier to dissolve if the documentation listed below is in place, than it is to liquidate a limited company in which you are jointly shareholders.

Partnership agreement
The partnership agreement sets up all the rules, responsibilities and financial details of a business partnership and its general partner. As noted earlier, each partner contributes to the equity of the partnership in cash or kind which could include office space or equipment. Profit and loss distribution can be specified on the basis of either:

- An equal share: each partner receives an equal amount of income and incurs equal liability for losses; or
- Fixed per cent: each partner receives a fixed proportion of gains or losses reflecting the agreed values of the relative contributions the partners anticipate.

To develop a sound partnership agreement you should include the following items in your contract:

- Partnership start date, name, address and purpose
- Contact details and duties of each general partner
- Description of partner capital contributions
- Who is responsible for the management of the business
- What meetings are to be held, voting rules and how decisions are to be made, including which decisions require unanimous partner consent
- Accounting methods and annual report details
- Profit and loss distribution (see above)
- Rules regarding the admission of new partners and withdrawal of existing partners
- Terms of a dissolution agreement (in Appendix) and rules for its enactment, including how assets and property will be divided if activated.

Serviceable template partnership agreement and dissolution contracts are offered free on the internet but you may feel more comfortable to make doubly sure by consulting a solicitor if there are any unusual features of your business or the partnership arrangements proposed.

LIMITED COMPANY DOCUMENTATION

The requirements of the Companies Act 2006 and the updated Regulations to the Act 2013 for the everyday running of a business are not too demanding and the facility for same day registration of a new company online through the Companies House website are among the reasons why non-residents choose to start up business in the UK rather than other territories.

Nevertheless, the formalities need to be strictly observed. Company registration and regular reporting are well monitored and failures to comply can be expensive and have negative effects on the reputations of the company and its directors.

Memorandum and Articles of Association
An important feature in the incorporation of any new company is the filing of its Memorandum and Articles of Association as an integral part of the registration process. Together they form the constitution of the company and set out the fundamental conditions under which the company is permitted to operate. The Memorandum (MOA) is basically a statement signed by the founding members (shareholders) of the company stating that they wish to form a company under the 2006 Companies Act, that they have agreed to become members, that it will have share capital and that they will each take at least one share. The MOA must also denote the name of the company, its head office, street address and names of (founding) directors. As a preliminary step, you should check that the company name you wish to adopt is available by checking online at https://www.gov.uk/choose-company-name. Both can be filed

from templates as part of the majority of available online registration services.

The Articles of Association are more detailed and are normally published and presented with the Memorandum as a single document. They define the purpose of the company and the kind of business to be undertaken (sometimes referred to as its "Objects"), the duties and responsibilities of its members, the duties and responsibilities of the directors and the means by which the shareholders exert control over the board of directors. The contents required under British Company Law include:

- The issuing of shares (also called stock) with different voting rights attached to different classes of shares
- Valuation of assets transferred to the company in exchange for shares (eg intellectual property rights or real estate)
- Transferability of shares – assignment rights of the founders or other members of the company, first right of refusal or counter-bid by the founder(s)
- The appointment of directors – showing whether one shareholder dominates or shares appointments equally with all the shareholders
- Meetings of shareholders – rules and procedures for how they are called and their conduct
- Special voting rights of a Chairman and how they are elected
- Management decisions – whether the board of directors or a founding member have authority
- The dividend policy – a percentage of profits to be declared (when there is a profit), by resolution of the shareholders at a general meeting, or otherwise
- Confidentiality of know-how – the founders' agreement and penalties for disclosure
- Winding up – conditions and notice to members.

The MOA or Articles of Association cannot be changed following registration except at an Annual General Meeting (AGM) or Extraordinary General Meeting (EGM).

Model Articles of Association
Most of these detailed matters will be of little concern to the founding members (owners) of start-up private limited companies. Rather than reinventing the wheel or agonizing over alternatives, owners usually adopt one of the model set of Articles of Association provided by the Registrar of Companies under the Companies Act. There are four samples labelled A, B, C and D respectively. Samples A and B are both designed for a private company, sample C for a public company and sample D for a company limited by guarantee.

Most private companies adopt the first version, generally known as Table A, and only think about amendment as the business develops and the need arises. However, I would advise that you check carefully that the purposes of the company, its Objects, are drawn sufficiently widely when you register the Articles of Association to encompass any kind of business that you are likely to undertake.

Registration
If not using an online service as above, you can register your private limited company online by visiting https://www.gov.uk/register-a-company-online and completing and submitting Form IN01 together with the Memorandum and Articles of Association. To complete Form IN01 you are required to enter:

- Name and address of the company (already entered in the MOA and Articles).
- Name and address of at least one director (and the company secretary, although this is now optional). Directors don't have to live in the UK but companies must have a UK registered office address. The

company secretary can be a director but not the company's auditor.

- Details of the company's shares: the number of shares of each class (maybe Preference Shares as well as Ordinary Shares) and their total value i.e. the company's "share capital".
  - * The price of a share can be any value. Shares can be issued part-paid but will have to be paid for in full if the company shuts down. For that reason, to limit future liability, you may choose a low share value (say £1) with an issued capital of 100 shares equal to £100.
  - * The rights of each class of share (referred to as "prescribed particulars") are defined in the Article of Association.
- The names and addresses of all shareholders (variously referred to as "subscribers" or "members") and the number of shares held by each shareholder.
- The company's SIC code. This is the standard industry classification used internationally, identifying the industry/business sector in which your company operates which you will find at https://www.gov.uk/government/publications/ standard-industrial-classification-of-economic-activities-sic

At the same time as you register the company, you must also register for Corporation Tax at: https://www.gov.uk/limited-company-formation/set-up-your-company-for-corporation-tax. This will be your first contact with HMRC in a corporate capacity, of which more in the next section and Chapter 6.

Companies House returns
Once a company is registered the directors are responsible for filing returns in respect of any change in the company's status or details including:

- Name
- Registered office
- Constitution (MMA or Articles)
- Directors and secretary
- Company records
- Resolutions
- Share capital
- Mortgages
- Strike off and dissolution

The form numbers and online filing details for each or these and more can be found at https://www.gov.uk/government/collections/companies-house-forms-for-limited-companies.

There are also two reports which have to be filed annually:

- Accounts at
  https://gov.uk/file-your-company-annual-accounts.
- Confirmation statement (Form CS01), formerly Annual Return (Form AR01) before 30 June 2016.

The weight of all this documentation is not as onerous as it seems at first sight since filing requirements are only periodic after the initial company registration. However, they can be a deterrent to incorporation if you can carry on your business successfully as a sole trader or in a limited liability partnership. When you do decide to incorporate it will help to conserve the use of your time if your domestic partner took on the role of Company Secretary. Be sure to ask nicely.

CHOOSING YOUR FINANCIAL YEAR END

The main considerations in choosing your financial year end are taxation related. I could have left this topic until Chapter 6, but the right choice can have a favourable effect on cashflow and therefore your funding requirements when we come to discuss them in the next Chapter. The situation for sole traders and partnerships is similar but differs for limited companies.

Sole traders and partnerships
As we noted earlier the profits and losses of sole traders and partners pass through to the individuals and are included in their personal tax assessments.

It follows that if you set the financial year-end of your business before 5th April the profit or loss of the previous trading year immediately preceding will be treated as personal income or loss for that tax year. Conversely, if you set the business's financial year-end after 5th April the results for that 12 month period will not be included in your personal tax return until the following year.

For example, if your first business year end is 31 March 2019, the outcome will be taken into account for your personal tax return for the 2018/19 tax year due before 31 January 2020. Alternatively, if your first business year is 30 April 2019, you will declare any profit or loss in your income tax return for the 2019/20 income tax due before 31 January 2021.

Of course, it's not quite as simple as that. Although first financial year can be either shorter or longer than 12 months, subsequent year ends will be at 12-month intervals. You can apply to change your financial year end in subsequent years but you will need to show a sufficient reason to satisfy HMRC.

Two other points should be taken into account:

- Once you have shown a positive income on your tax return, HMRC will set a mid-year amount of tax for the next year which you will be required to pay on account and which will be adjusted annually in relation to your reported income each year.

- Year end losses on your business may be offset against any other income and unused losses may be carried forward to the next year. This might be relevant if you have left employment mid-year and tax has been deducted by PAYE from your salary. If the sum is sufficiently large and your business has shown a loss in its early months you might choose to take 31 March as the financial year end in order to recover tax paid.

I am not an accountant and if you already have one or know someone who is you would be wise to take advice in order to be sure that you make the decision which will benefit you most.

Limited companies

The timing issues for limited companies are more complex, but it is easier to shorten or lengthen the accounting year at will by completing and submitting a change of account reference date return (Form AA01) at the website referenced above. One reason for lengthening the reference date may be that the accounts have not yet been prepared pending completion of a transaction that will have a material effect on the profit and loss account or balance sheet. The most obvious personal consideration is the timing of dividend payments which will impact shareholders' tax returns.

There is also flexibility in the timing of the annual confirmation statement to Companies House which will remain twelve months from the original date established at incorporation. There is an online filing fee of £13 for the first statement (£40 in hard copy) and additional statements may be filed to record significant changes during the year without charge. The timing for filing the next statement is extended to 12 months following any mid-year filing.

Penalties and deterrents

If a private company's first accounts cover a period of more than 12 months they must be presented to Companies House within 21 months of the date of incorporation. In subsequent years, a private company must deliver its accounts within 9 months of the accounting reference period.

The level of penalty for late delivery of private company accounts is determined by how late the accounts reach Companies House according to the following scale:

Not more than 1 month	£150
More than 1 month but not more than 3 months	£375
More than 3 months but not more than 6 months	£750
More than 6 months	£1,500

In the event of accounts being filed late for two successive years the penalties are doubled.

When the annual confirmation statement is not filed on time, notice that it is outstanding is posted on its Companies House file. After warnings to the directors and a further period of normally 6 months, the company may no longer trade if the statement has not been filed and is struck off the register.

A practical deterrent to all late filing is that the company's shortcomings are readily exposed to anyone searching the Companies House register. If you are pitching for business with important new clients or looking for credit from your suppliers, this exposure indicating that the company is poorly administered or suggesting that it is in financial difficulty may have an adverse effect.

All of these regulations are in the interest of maximum transparency in the conduct of corporate business. Never let it be said of your company, as it was in the 1711 prospectus for The South Sea Company:

"A Company for carrying on an undertaking of Great Advantage, but no one to knows what it is."

– Cowles, The Great Swindle, (1963), ch 5

4

FUNDING YOUR BUSINESS

"Neither a borrower, nor a lender be;
For loan oft loses both itself and friend,
And borrowing dulls the edge of husbandry…"

– Polonius, Hamlet, William Shakespeare (1564-1616)

CASHFLOW IS KING – HOW MUCH DO YOU NEED?

You may think that the quotation is a curious choice with which to begin a chapter about raising money to start your business, but all will be revealed as we go along. After many years' experience of success – and failure – in financing businesses from start-up to merger or flotation, I draw three conclusions:

- Raising funds for start-ups present the greatest challenge.
- At each stage of a developing business, don't take more cash from investors than you realistically need.
- Whenever possible, for start-ups take in investment rather than borrow.

Let's make a first pass at each point before deliberating on the alternative forms of finance that may be available.

Funds for start-ups present the greatest challenge

The key constraints on what you can hope to achieve are project credibility and your personal track record. If you have carried out the planning process thoroughly and the business concept remains intact, you will have gone a long way to satisfy project credibility and a well-considered structure which you articulate clearly is a good first step in establishing your credibility as an independent businessperson.

However, your personal track record may not convince potential investors or lenders that you have an entrepreneurial mindset. Showing your absolute conviction that the business you are about start is financially and operationally viable is essential but what can you demonstrate from your past career and experience that will enhance the confidence of others? Past employment in management roles may be impressive but will not suffice without evidence of several of the following:

- Project management responsibility
- Initiative and innovation in introducing new products or services
- Successful management of loss-making turn-around situations
- Risk-taking and you came through successfully
- Leadership of change management programmes

If you can't demonstrate sufficient achievements in your past working life, look beyond to activities in social and charity work or sport where your activities in the community demonstrate the same qualities. Past experience of a start-up which failed is not necessarily fatal, but do not attempt to cover it up. Be ready to comment on the experience when challenged and the lessons that you have learnt from it.

In all contacts with people and organisations that might back you, be sure to show confidence but not arrogance and, above all, prepare yourself to address any of the issues raised above.

Don't take more cash than you need
The focus on cashflow forecasting in Chapter 2 enables you to estimate the funding which you will need before your business becomes cash positive and this will determine the amount of funding you will need if everything goes according to plan. It is sensible to add to this sum a provision for additional working capital if the progress of the business is delayed. My advice is to build in an allowance for a further three months before the business achieves break-even and becomes cash neutral. On the other hand, do not over-provide for three reasons:

1. When you show your business plan to potential backers, it will be readily apparent how much you need to get the business off the ground and over-egging your funding requirement will make a poor impression. It will suggest either that you have little confidence in your plan or, worse, that you don't intend to "run a tight ship".
2. By the time that your start-up has taken more than three months to achieve equilibrium and you are unable to delay expenditure or accelerate income you should have adjusted your plan accordingly or taken it back to the drawing board. You may even have to consider ceasing to trade.
3. It is also true that surplus cash may lead to profligacy: unnecessary items of expenditure, giving additional credit to customers by failing to enforce your payment terms, *pro bono* work to gain business or simply taking more money out of the business than you should.

Take in investment rather than borrow
If you have family or friends who are eager to back you take it rather than borrow externally. For the reasons set out try to take the cash support as an investment rather than a loan. I acknowledge that this is a personal preference based on

my experience, but my reasoning is that as your business expands you may need more working capital and you are more likely to negotiate a suitable facility with your bank if you can show that you have had investor support from the outset.

Having taken my strictures on board, you are now ready to explore alternative sources of funding.

ALTERNATIVE SOURCES OF FUNDING

Own funds
Unless you are starting your business while you are still employed, or have some alternative source of significant income, you are unlikely to be able to sustain the cash outflow of a new business, even if there is no fixed capital requirement. In any case, "moonlighting" is a poor way to start your own business beyond initial market testing. It will certainly detract from the attention you pay to your day job and thereby short change your employer to some degree. And setting aside any ethical considerations, a start-up business with any decent chance of success demands the full time input of its owner-managers.

If you have some liquid capital in the form of cash at the bank or securities that will be available subject to the agreement of your immediate family, consider using these resources first. If you are due a redundancy lump sum from previous employment it can be deployed in the start-up period with a clear conscience but think very carefully before cashing in any part of your occupational pension entitlement. Reducing your future unearned income in retirement is not very sensible; you would probably regret it later.

Of the four examples first cited in Chapter 1, Fred may be able to start his plumbing business from scratch with a little tightening of the belt. He has the advantage that his customers may be happy to pay on completion of each job and no significant overhead expense is incurred other than the operating cost of his van.

Alice may also be able to get her PR business off the ground without looking for third party finance, particularly since she has one major client on monthly retainer, but will find it hard to expand her role beyond that of a personal consultant to a handful of clients without setting up an office with at least one member of staff.

Simon's Case C project to launch a remote control fuel tank cap will certainly require outside funding and the real life Case D online IP transaction platform needed substantial funding from the outset to develop the architecture of its internet platform.

Family and friends

Borrowing money from friends is hazardous and risks broken friendship as Shakespeare's Polonius observes and borrowing from family members is often worse. The problem is that it is seldom treated as an arm's length business transaction. The borrower is placing themselves under an ongoing obligation to someone or people that he/she sees in daily social life and will feel guilty if repayment is not made on time. The lender, unless an exceptional friend or very trusting relative, will probably have a sense of entitlement ranging from a tendency to interfere in the running of the business to a belief that granting the loan is equivalent to taking a share in the business. If the latter, and the business does well, the lender may well expect to receive a share of the profits or proceeds of any sale over and above repayment in full. Conversely, if the business fails the lender may still expect to receive their money back in full.

The only way to mitigate, if not eliminate, the relationship problem is to draw up a formal legal agreement, to be signed by both parties, which sets out explicitly the terms and conditions of the loan, any interest charged and repayment. The alternative which I prefer personally, if acceptable to the provider, is to take the funds as an investment, to incorporate and to issue shares in exchange. Provided that you remain the majority shareholder, preferably with more than 75% of the issued capital, this will work better than a loan. Taking the provider in as a general or limited liability partner is a less acceptable alternative as it entails a greater involvement in the day to day business than you would wish.

There is a halfway house between lending and direct investment in the form of convertible loans. A friend of mine who was given the opportunity to buy an embryo internet company of which he had led the development needed to bring in additional funding to complete the acquisition. He turned to a former work colleague and longstanding friend to provide financial support and play a part in the business. The arrangement agreed between them was that the friend would put up the money as a cash loan with rights to convert the whole or a part into a minority shareholding. I was happy to draft the formal agreement between them. In the event, a major part of the loan was converted when a substantial external investment was received. Ultimately, both friends recovered the amounts of their investments on resale to another investor and are still talking to each other.

I shall have more to say later in this chapter about convertible loan instruments in the context of structured finance in private equity investment and structured finance in general. Both have their uses.

DEBT FINANCE

Before you embark on any approach to a bank or other lender the first step is to check your credit rating on line with leading credit agencies Experian and Equifax. A poor score will make the task of raising a loan harder, sometimes impossible. All County Court judgements or any breach of a credit agreement that the lender chooses to register will show up on your record. The latter may prove fatal to your lending application. You can check your credit record yourself through Experian or Equifax (it might be worth verifying which service the bank uses) and speak to them about removing defaults if you can evidence that they were made in error.

Bank borrowing

With a clean credit record and fairly modest requirements your first port of call will be the bank with which you hold your personal account and may already have an overdraft or personal loan. As discussed in Chapter 2, you will probably need a current account for the business as a sole trader; if you form a partnership or a limited company you will certainly need a new account in the business's name. Therefore, a discussion with your bank is a sensible first step.

For Alice's PR business and Fred's plumbing business a simple overdraft renewable annually may be enough, but if they were looking for more than £5,000 credit, their banks would probably offer a personal or business loan, and facilities up to £25,000 are widely available for those businesses satisfying bank criteria. If your business is more like Simon's Case C or the internet platform project of Case D, both involving an innovative product or service, you will almost certainly need substantially more than £25,000, you can skip the rest of this section, scan the section on asset finance and move on to the final sections of this chapter relating to private equity.

Business loans are easier to negotiate with banks for established companies with a decent track record and, perhaps, an asset base. Part of the problem is that the "negotiation" process is minimal and consists largely of inputted data and responses online, either in person at the bank by a customer service adviser with you in attendance or remotely by phone. The bank's responses are wholly formulaic and, although there may be a token appeals procedure, bank decisions are inflexible. In days of yore, branch bank managers had limits of authority to apply their own judgements when decision making or recommending approval for loan applications. Today they have little or no influence on the computerised decision process. You may conclude in today's idiom, as I have done, that the automated intelligence that banks apply to their decision making really is "artificial".

The terms of bank business loans vary but, typically, you may expect:

- Repayment usually restricted to no more than 3 – 5 years with regular interest and repayment instalments.
- Sometimes, but more rarely today, a payment holiday of up to 6 months with the accrued interest recovered over subsequent instalments.
- Possibly, a commitment fee when the loan is taken out deductible from the amount advanced.
- In the case of a company, a fixed and floating charge over its assets.
- In the case of partnerships or limited companies, personal guarantees from general partners or company directors.

The climate of historically low interest rates immediately following the 2008 financial crash has come to an end, as banks have lowered their risk appetites, with interest rates on commercial loans likely to continue rising moderately over the next twelve months. Nevertheless, bank borrowing remains the most attractive form of debt finance for small companies. Indeed, it is sometimes sensible to put additional overdraft facilities in place when you can and delay using them because a bank is less likely to agree an overdraft when problems arise and you really need it.

However, if your only asset of substance is your house, already mortgaged, and you have no favourable credit history with the bank, you may be asked to allow a second charge to be registered on the property. You will need to consult carefully with your family before agreeing, even if the house is in your sole ownership. Family relationships can be broken irrevocably in the event that you are called upon to pay off and you do not have their consent.

Asset finance

Asset-based finance looks primarily at the value of a specific asset rather than overall balance sheet strength as in floating charges for bank borrowing. For a start-up business like yours leasing is the most likely form of asset finance which can supplement bank borrowing unless the finance house is a part of the bank. In that case, the leasing arrangement may have an impact on the amount that the bank will loan.

Leasing is easiest to arrange for assets where market value is readily assessed such as motor vehicles, manufacturing, business and IT equipment. The advantages for the lessee are:

- Funding is available for the total cost of the asset;
- Depreciation and losses on re-sale are avoided;
- Depending on the circumstances of the lessee in respect of tax, VAT and capital allowances, some leasing structures have a cost advantage over a bank loan (You will need to calculate comparative costs carefully and, if you are uncertain, take an accountant's advice).

The negative points in leasing are obvious:

- Interest charges on which the monthly rental is based, together with estimated end-of-lease residual value, are higher than the interest rates of bank borrowing.
- Early termination is expensive involving penalty charges and re-calculation of residual value at that time.
- No balance sheet value for the asset is created over the period of the lease.

Against these disadvantages old-fashioned hire purchase has its attractions. Interest rates are also higher than for bank loans but early termination is less onerous (simply a matter of repaying principal plus outstanding interest.)

For motor vehicles the auto manufacturers and their finance companies have come up with ingenious hybrid deals classified as lease purchase. Under most of these the lessee makes a down payment and then pays a fixed monthly charge over a period of two to four years, compounded of interest and principal to cover the calculated depreciation in value during the period of the lease. At the end of the lease period you have the option to return the vehicle or purchase at the pre-agreed contract price. The main purpose of these offers is to tempt the customer into acquiring a more expensive prestige make or model than you would have chosen otherwise.

However confident you may be that your start-up will flourish during the contract period, don't yield to this temptation; it will count against you when you come to negotiate business borrowing. Clients won't be impressed either; they may consider that that they are subsidising your lifestyle at their expense through higher fees.

Factoring
Factoring or invoice discounting can be a useful tool for accelerating the inward cashflow of smaller companies, whereby the finance company advances you a proportion of your outstanding invoices and takes on the financial risk and responsibility for collection. The lender looks to the quality of the trade debtors as security rather than overall balance sheet assets so that the debt element becomes "off balance sheet". The amounts advanced can be as much as 90% of the face value of invoices less finance charges depending on the quality of the debts and the arrangement is a rolling facility as accounts are paid and more invoices are raised. A factoring company can be part of a bank or a specialist company that

may refinance itself by the block discounting of invoices accepted. Either way the interest charges are higher than straightforward bank borrowing.

Clearly this form of financing is not available to your business at the time of start-up. It applies only when you have built up a sufficient level of business, normally not less than 18 months later when you are also able to show your first year's accounts. You need to be confident that your business is growing or at least maintaining a steady level of sales. If not, as the draw down from discounted invoices rolls through you will find yourself in a further cash squeeze.

Of our four start-up examples, only Alice's Case A PR business is likely to be eligible for factoring in its second year as its range of quality clients is extended. However, all invoice discounting carries the disadvantage that the finance house will want to interpose its identity, however discreetly, in collecting payment and, for a business like Alice's, that may be a problem. Signalling that your invoices have been factored may be taken as an indication that your business is cash poor and will detract from your company's standing.

Alternative lending facilities
There is one further kind of debt finance which is not strictly asset-based and which applies only to businesses which have some trading record. Described sometimes as a "revolving credit facility" it is the business equivalent of consumer payday lending and, perhaps unfairly, is tarred with the same brush of negative comment. The way it works is that the credit provider, having assessed eligibility and risk, offers an advance, say £10,000, repayable in full by instalments over a fixed period, normally 12 months. The borrower can repay more than the minimum monthly instalment and, subject to the lender's agreement, can top up the debt to £10,000. Not unexpectedly, interest rates are high, typically 3.7% per 30 days on the outstanding balance. Therefore, on a £10,000 loan after 30 days with no early repayments, the amount

payable to the finance house would be £1,203 and, after 60 days, a further £1,083.

An arrangement fee is usually charged, but decisions are made quickly, typically within 48 hours on the basis of three months' bank statements and the latest company accounts.

This is a dangerous way to fund your business except for short term emergencies and then only when you are confident of stronger forward cashflow. Revolving credit facilities for SMEs are likely to also involve personal guarantees from the company's directors.

GRANTS

A key funding source for UK businesses is Innovate UK (formerly the Strategy Board) which was formed in 2008. Its various programmes for companies of any sector and size are intended to support businesses in their R&D activities. For technical feasibility studies and industrial research small businesses may apply for a maximum 70% of total cost up to £100,000 for a feasibility stage project and up to £1million for a development stage project. The Small Business Research Initiative (SBRI), which is where you would start, operates on scheduled timings to apply for a SMART grant with several tranches each year. Response times are good, usually within one month of each closing date.

To be eligible, your project needs to demonstrate highly innovative processes, products or services that have the potential to deliver significant business growth. It follows that neither Alice's PR business nor Fred's home maintenance service could apply with any chance of success and Simon's remote control fuel tank cap project would struggle for acceptance.

The real life company (Case D) did apply for a feasibility stage grant to research the market for its IP transfer internet platform and was successful. It was awarded £20,000, having shown that it had committed financial support of £42,000 from its shareholders to cover the balance of the cost of its pre-start up activity. (Some cost elements were not eligible for consideration in the grant calculation).

Other grants are available for specific sectors such as bio-medical, agri-tech and energy under the Catalyst Programmes run jointly by Innovate UK and the Research Councils. Full information for all Innovate UK managed funding programmes can be found at https://www.gov.uk/apply-funding-innovation.

Research funding grants for UK SMEs have also been available under EUREKA Eurostars, a joint programme between the European Union and more than 30 EUREKA member countries, but continued eligibility for UK companies is uncertain until Brexit negotiations are completed.

USING ADVISERS

Having revisited earlier books that I have written about starting up and running businesses I can see that I used to advise entrepreneurs to consult professional advisers long before this stage of preparation and planning. For this book, so far I have advocated taking professional advice only in connection with taxation issues and in drawing up partnership and shareholder agreements. The reasons for this are twofold:

- Thanks to the internet, it has become easy to research every aspect of doing business, even to download model agreements, accountancy workbooks and spreadsheets prepared by qualified professionals for your immediate use.
- It is no longer particularly useful to take your accountant with you to the bank when opening a business account or arranging an overdraft or loan. As noted earlier in this chapter, the decision-making

authority or influence of bank managers over borrowing decisions is so limited that relationships between local bank managers and accountants, however cordial, are largely irrelevant.

Of course, I am not advising you *not* to take legal or accountancy advice if you feel uncomfortable, but the cost of professional support can be deferred up to this point. When you are embarking on a search for investors and intend to engage with them, however, you will need the support of professionals.

The rest of this chapter is not really relevant if your business is of similar size or nature to either Case A or Case B of our Chapter One examples. Unless your business plan anticipates high growth and you are looking for a minimum of £100,000 now with the prospect of more in the medium-term you are unlikely to attract the attention of equity funds or venture capitalists other than solo business angels. Both Case C and Case D fall within these parameters.

Selecting advisers
There are directories of financial advisers registered as qualified with the Financial Conduct Authority (FCA) but nearly all of them are practising advisers to consumers on pensions, insurance, mortgages or equity release. The adviser you choose now may or may not be professionally qualified in the law or accountancy; you will certainly need a solicitor when you have an outline offer, subject to contract, to take the deal forward with the investor's lawyers and you will probably need an accountant to help you respond to due diligence enquiries. However, in finding a compatible investor and negotiating the deal any adviser you appoint now will need to demonstrate to you both successful experience and access channels to those sectors of the investor community with an interest in financing start-ups.

You may be fortunate in having friends or business acquaintances who have been through the funding process successfully with guidance from a financial adviser whom they will recommend to you and who will serve you equally well. But there are pitfalls and you must take care not to fall into the hands of charlatans. A first test is the adviser's terms of business. Good advisers to start-up entrepreneurs will expect payment by results in the form of commission in cash or new shares in your company – probably a higher rate if they have found the investor (better described as a "finder's fee") and a lower rate or fixed fee if they are advising, at your request, on an approach from an investor whom you have sourced yourself. Be alert to the following unreasonable demands:

- *Upfront fees* – For established businesses, usually listed companies, investment bank advisers commonly have pre-agreed fees payable if negotiations fail, but that is not appropriate to your situation. You might consider modest out of pocket expenses but nothing more.
- *Shares in your company* – As an incentive to broker the best deal available for your company, shares rather than cash seems an attractive way of paying for advice and could be acceptable if you foresee a continuing relationship with the adviser. But bear in mind that you will be issuing shares to investors, possibly up to 30% of your company's equity and you will want to retain control. You may also want to issue shares to your key staff in time.
- *Joining the board* – Any invitation to serve as a director of your company is within your gift until you bring in an outside investor, but you should not consider any self-serving proposal from an adviser to be appointed.
- *Fees for advice other than finder's fees* – Avoid paying for advice which you have not requested. It's easy to be trapped. Several years ago, a friend of mine was introduced by a recommended adviser to a colleague, later identified as his partner, who made a convincing pitch that he would find an investor and advise on the

deal. No upfront fee was requested, only commission at 5% of the amount raised. My friend signed the adviser's standard terms of business. After some months without any introductions, my friend himself approached a major US company in a similar line of business who made a substantial investment offer which he accepted and the deal was done without any reference to the adviser. Nevertheless, the adviser claimed fees of 5%, amounting to more than £20,000, on the grounds that he had been appointed to advise on any deal whether or not he had found the investor and that he should have been consulted. Solicitors' advice to my friend was that the cleverly worded terms of business could be construed in that way and advised him to negotiate a settlement. Subsequently the original recommended adviser, who received a share of the settlement fee, was blackballed by the clients who had introduced him, but that was cold comfort for an expensive five-figure outcome.

With that cautionary tale in mind you may decide to find an investor yourself unaided and to negotiate an offer as far as possible without using an adviser. The next section will tell you how to identify potential investors and how to attract attention.

EQUITY AND STRUCTURED FINANCE INVESTORS

For start-up businesses looking for substantial funds there are four alternative avenues to search:

- Business angels
- Venture capitalists
- Private equity
- Crowdfunding

The first three categories are not rigidly compartmentalised. Some groups of private investors who function as angels define themselves as private equity providers as do some venture capitalists. Crowdfunding is a distinct category which has emerged quite recently and provides direct access to a consumer market of small private investors whose decisions to back a new product or service are taken by individual amateur investors.

I will try first to share with you my understanding of each of the first three categories and how to identify them before moving on to how best to pique their interest. In the penultimate section of this chapter I will give you a brief introduction to crowdfunding.

The first thing to understand is the common mindset of all three categories of investor:

- All three start out with the expectation that no more than 30% of their investments will be successful. Therefore, they look for high returns from those that prosper.
- Most business angels and venture capitalists aim to exit their investment within 3 to 4 years. Some business angels playing an active part in the management of an investment and larger equity funds may take a longer view.
- Attractive investments are based on "scaleability", a concept beloved by business school graduates and meaning that the target company operates in a market niche and with a business plan that shows geometric growth rates.
- Before securing investment you will need to show evidence, known as "proof of concept", that your product is commercially viable and will make money.

Simon should have little difficulty in satisfying this test for his innovative Case C fuel tank cap because the product has already been launched successfully in Australia. Proof of concept was the hurdle for our Case D IP transaction internet platform which proved ultimately unsurmountable.

- Among the various yardsticks for measuring the investor's return on investment is the "Internal Rate of Return" (IRR) favoured by private equity. In effect it is the return from the investment in terms of cash received from dividends over the life of the investment plus the cash recovered at the end of the investment from the sale of shares, net of tax and discounted by the time intervals before receipt, expressed as a percentage of the original investment. Another common business plan measurement tool, compatible with IRR, is EBITDA – earnings before interest on debt, corporation tax, depreciation and amortisation.

Don't attempt to make the IRR calculation for your business plan yourself – potential investors will do that themselves using their own projections for dividend rates and share sale price. Just be sure to provide a line in your projections showing the company's cumulative cashflow.

- UK business angels individually are motivated to invest in unlisted SMEs by tax benefits of the government's Enterprise Investment Scheme (EIS) and, particularly in start-ups, by the Seed Enterprise Investment Scheme (SEIS). In both cases they will, after the end of three years, when taking profits from the sale of an investment, have exemption from capital gains tax (CGT). EIS investments under £1 million enjoy 30% income tax relief and under SEIS the relief is extended to 50%. Anyone receiving income from the company is ineligible as are shareholders with more than 30% of the issued capital.

Angel investors
Aside from the availability of tax incentives the distinguishing characteristics of business angels are that they are usually wealthy businesspersons favouring early-stage investments.

Often they have successful businesses themselves which became the source of their present wealth. Therefore, they are able to offer their expertise and experience to your business and are often keen to be involved. They will understand from their first-hand experience the pressures and problems of starting a business. Their involvement in your business may be a plus or negative depending on personal empathy and your tolerance of possible interference.

Usually their individual investment is likely to be between £10,000 and £100,000 and they tend to hunt in groups through networks. For example, the Oxford Investment Opportunity Network (OION) forms a new investment company for each tax year through which individuals may invest as a syndicate to take advantage of SEIS relief. It has its own management team that selects a portfolio of early stage companies in each of which the consortium of angel investors take shares. The OION consortia are more likely to invest in straight equity than a mixture of shares and debt instruments. There is a preference for innovative high-tech projects. For example, our Case D IP transaction platform received an offer of support funding from OION conditional upon securing primary funding within that tax year but this was the point at which the project stalled.

Venture capitalists
Focused on companies that already have some track record rather than start-ups, venture capitalists operate on a professional basis and their investment level is normally in excess of £250,000 and can extend to several million. They are investment companies in their own right with professional management teams and are more demanding in terms of proof of concept, experienced management and detailed research on markets, competition and opportunities. They are likely to offer funding packages in which most of the money is provided by loans or in preference shares with fixed redemption dates and only a small proportion as permanent share capital.

Private equity funds

Although both business angels and venture capitalists operate under the broad private equity banner, I prefer to reserve the private equity fund label for the larger investment companies that provide multi-million-pound funding and sometimes involve themselves in corporate rescues and acquisitions. Note that both venture capital and private equity investors, while often investing substantial amounts, will have clear target exit dates in mind, usually within 5 and often within 3 years and may withdraw support or try to force a sale to recover some of their investment if the target looks unlikely to be achieved.

Identifying potential investors

There is no difficulty in identifying either business angel networks or venture capitalists, the former by visiting the website of the UK Business Angels Association at www.ukbaa.org.uk and the latter at www.bvca.co.uk. Confusingly, venture capitalists claim to be represented also in the BAA membership and that the BVCA membership includes equity funds which emphasises how the categories overlap. You will have to request access to the membership lists and you will then be able to filter the lists yourself.

Other angel syndicates similar to OION are identifiable through the business studies department of leading universities who host their own angel networks. They each have their own selection parameters and ground rules which are readily identifiable through direct communication.

Alternatively you will find lists of angel networks and venture capital investors in David Bateman's new *Investment Handbook*, also published by Legend Business Books.

Attracting attention

The first step is to make contact with potential investors and send them an electronic copy of your business plan, being sure to follow the KISS parameters mentioned in Chapter 2. I make no excuse for advising you to follow the formats and models set out in David Bateman's first book *Business Plans that Get Investment*. The templates for each page can be downloaded off the same website. Remember that your objective is to open the door to discussion supported then by your more detailed planning documents and projections. Anything more at this stage is likely to be a turn-off. The covering email should be short and sufficient to stimulate the opening of the attachment and provide your contact details but no more.

I can vouch for the effectiveness of the approach. Using David Bateman's format and page models the approach to OION for investment in our IP transaction internet platform drew a rapid response and the opportunity to present to their angel network with coaching on how to make the presentation.

Having contacted your chosen potential investors, if you receive no reply within a week, follow up by telephone. Cold calling is always a somewhat daunting experience but you will find that this is not like selling a product or service. The responses you receive will be polite and often friendly. Remember that you are inviting participation in your business and that is an opportunity for their business which commands respect.

Crowdfunding

It is said that there are now more than 2,000 crowdfunding websites in operation enabling investment pitches to be made to the general public. The leading websites include Kickstarter, Indiegogo, Crowdcube and Seedrs. Some of them. like Crowdcube. specialise in consumer products and services with wide business to consumer appeal (B2C). Others, such as Seedrs, are targeted at business investors with B2B offerings.

Crowdfunding success depends on achieving the minimum targeted level of investment pledges within a limited time and crowdfunders, when taking on an investment project, emphasise that a significant level of advance pledges that can be visible online is a necessary pre-condition for stimulating the rapid growth of an investment following. The downside of using crowdfunding is that it is an unrepeatable exercise if the first attempt fails. And crowdfunding failure is likely to have an adverse effect on generating investment interest from more conventional sources. Many businesses have used crowdfunding successfully but note that while the business plan and numbers are obviously vital, its nature means those with an existing online, social media or business following that can be tapped into are the most likely to succeed.

CONTINUING THE INVESTMENT JOURNEY

The rest of your investment journey through negotiating terms and evaluating the merits of investment offers and the implications of investor involvement in your business are beyond the scope of this book but I have included a section on living with their outcome in Chapter 6.

However, this is as good a time as any to advise caution. Looking before you leap into any deal with investors is essential and helping you to do that is an important part of a professional adviser's role. You are not obliged to accept any investment offer you may receive, however hard you have fought for it. There is a tendency to accept with relief when negotiations have been prolonged, but do not close a more cynical eye too soon. There is always an alternative.

"Do not trust the horse, Trojans. Whatever it is, I fear
The Greeks, even when they bring gifts."

– Virgil, 70-19 B.C.

5

BASIC ACCOUNTING
AND TAXATION

"To give an accurate and exhaustive account of that period would need a far less brilliant pen than mine."

– Max Beerbohm, 1872-1956

And so it is for most of us who find accountancy and taxation boring but necessary routines that demand accurate and exhaustive record keeping. When you start, you will want to do the minimum necessary to keep your business safe and under control and I have addressed both topics together in this chapter. Your accountant, when you employ one, may not approve wholly of my advice; it is based on the experience of many years when I have had financial responsibility for my own business and also been expected to bring sound judgement as a non-executive director to the accounts of companies and charities on whose boards I have served.

THE AMATEUR ACCOUNTANT

The art of coarse accountancy that I advocate can be practised by amateur accountants with confidence that they will not put their businesses at undue risk and that your records will satisfy third party scrutiny.

In my youth I was brought up on a diet of double entry bookkeeping and trial balances based on day books and ledgers, all maintained manually, both time-consuming and tiresome. Today, you can forget that kind of bean counting exercise. By the time the business has developed to the point where formal Profit and Loss and Balance Sheet accounts are needed, you will be able to use one of the digitally operated software packages, of which more later, that require little more than the input of cash book entries, your invoices and the invoices of suppliers and subcontractors. They will then churn out all the financial statements and reports that you would normally need.

Bear in mind only the three basic legal requirements to:

- Set up adequate records of all business transactions, including personal drawings and personal money put into the business.
- Maintain those records throughout the year and keep them up to date.
- Retain the documentation for a recommended six years.

CASHFLOW FORECASTING AND REVISION

Let's begin by returning to a favourite theme of this book which runs like the logo through a stick of Blackpool rock: cashflow and its day to day management.

It has been said that more than 80 per cent of business failures are caused by inadequate record keeping. I think we can drill down to the root cause. Most business bankruptcies are the result of cashflow failure. And if that sounds a bit like putting heart failure as "cause of death" on a doctor's certificate, I mean something more specific. Of course, any entrepreneur who allows expenditure to exceed revenue for any length of time will face liquidation of their business and, maybe worse if personal guarantees are involved, but that is avoidable. By forecasting and monitoring cashflow rigorously, you can usually curtail expenditure commitments in time to avert disaster when order income and therefore revenue fails to keep pace.

The tools for forecasting and monitoring cashflow are:

- A spreadsheet that forecasts all items of revenue (cash received not invoices) and all significant expenses to be paid which you update regularly for actual receipts and amounts paid and roll forward your forecast on revised expectations. It is best to forecast forward by 12 months on a frequency of one month or, better still, week by week. Those with a taste for number crunching may choose to forecast day by day.
- Bank account entries for actual receipt and payments which can be checked daily online.

If this discipline seems too daunting, the burden is eased by using Excel sheets downloadable on your PC or desktop on which corrections can be carried through automatically at the stroke of a key. (I enclose a sample spreadsheet using notional numbers for Alice's PR agency.)

The last three lines of the spreadsheet are the most informative, showing net cash inflow or outflow for each period and, ultimately, the cumulative cash position in terms of the opening and closing balance for each period. If you have mastered Excel spreadsheet formulas, addition and subtraction will be carried out automatically.

FIGURE 5.1 ALICE GOODFELLOW – CASH FLOW FORECAST

Year 1 – Month	1	2	3	4	5	6	7	8	9	10	11	12	total
	£	£	£	£	£	£	£	£	£	£	£	£	£
SALES REVENUE (excl VAT)													
Retainers													
Gibson, Granger & Halliday		750	1220	750	750	750	750	750	750	750	750	750	8,720
DesRes Estate Agents				400	400	400	400	400	400	400	400	400	3,600
Micro Autowidgets						800	800	800	800	800	800	800	5,600
Help the Hopeless							600	600	600	1050	600	600	4,050
Invoiced fees & reinvoiced costs													
Medusa Hair Salons			750	370			430			640		210	2,400
Cutprice Car Auctions					1700					1550			3,250
HiLevel Escorts				700		350		1200			700		2,400
Killjoy Funeral Directors							600	600	600		600		2,830
Sayonara Sushi						500	500		500	500		830	2,830
Total Sales Revenue (excl. VAT)		750	1970	2220	2850	2800	4080	4350	3650	5690	3850	3590	35,800
VAT invoiced							*(When registered for VAT from year 2 onwards)*						
Total Revenue Received		**750**	**1970**	**2220**	**2850**	**2800**	**4080**	**4350**	**3650**	**5690**	**3850**	**3590**	**35,800**

81

FIGURE 5.1 ALICE GOODFELLOW – CASH FLOW FORECAST (continued)

Year 1 – Month	1	2	3	4	5	6	7	8	9	10	11	12	total
EXPENDITURE (incl. VAT paid)	£	£	£	£	£	£	£	£	£	£	£	£	£
Direct debits and standing orders	225	225	225	225	225	225	225	225	225	225	225	225	2,700
Bank charges and interest	300	300	300	300	300	300	300	300	300	300	300	300	3,600
Payments to subcontractors & suppliers	1200		470		600			450		750		330	3,800
Staff fees and salaries		500	500	500	500	500	500	750	750	750	750	750	6,750
Heating & lighting	110	110	110	110	110	185	185	185	185	185	185	135	1,795
Telephone & internet			140			170			190			210	710
Motor car petrol & oil	130	130	130	150	150	150	170	170	170	200	200	200	1,950
Motor car maintenance & repairs									300				300
MOT, RFL & AA membership	125				120								245
Other travel costs			70		70		70	80	80	80	60	70	580
Self-payments		1000	1000	1000	1000	1500	1500	1500	1500	2000	2000	2000	16,000
Total expenditure (incl. VAT paid)	2090	2265	2945	2285	3075	3030	2950	3660	3700	4490	3720	4220	38,430
VAT paid on inputs				*(Deductible against VAT invoiced on sales from Year 2 when registered)*									
PAYE and NI on salaries						*(When incorporated from Year 2)*							
Total Payments	2090	2265	2945	2285	3075	3030	2950	3660	3700	4490	3720	4220	38,430
NET CASH FLOW	-2090	-1515	-975	-165	225	230	1320	690	-50	2200	130	360	
CUMULATIVE CASH FLOW	-2090	-3605	-4580	-4745	-4520	-4290	-2970	-2280	-2330	-130	-	360	

Alice's assessments

When Alice prepared her original cashflow forecast she didn't know who her clients would be except for the first client on retainer, her old employer Gibson Granger & Halliday, who awarded her a 12 month contract to service her old clients for which she had been the account manager. However, she calculated that the monthly revenue she would need to generate to cover her expenditure and provide a minimal income for herself in the first 6 months would be at the level of £3,000 (including the retainer of £750 per month). Figure 5.1 is an illustration of how it might turn out.

Before discussing the numbers, an explanation of the format will help you to apply the same approach to your business:

- *Sales revenue* – Alice chooses to group her clients into those on a monthly retainer basis and those who commission her services according to monthly need. You may prefer to group your sales by industry sector or the salesman/account manager responsible for handling each customer (note that in month 3 Alice also receives payment from Gibson Granger & Halliday for the subcontracted website development work invoiced in month 2).

- *Provision for VAT* – I've included separate lines for VAT charged to clients (not included in sales revenue per client) and for VAT payable on purchases where applicable. There are no VAT entries on this sheet because Alice's Year 1 sales are well below the level where registration is compulsory. However, the expenditure entries include all VAT paid since those amounts are paid in the course of business. (More about VAT management later in this chapter).

- *PAYE* – The expenditure line for PAYE is also blank because Alice has elected for self-employment and her only member of staff is Agatha, whom she pays part-time as an administrative assistant below the PAYE and national insurance baseline.

- *Cash balances* – The last two lines record cashflow (revenue less expenditure) and cumulative cashflow month by month. You can add a further line to show "Closing Balance" if you start off with a positive balance in your bank account. In Alice's case she negotiated a £6,000 business loan with her bank so her current account at the end of the first month would show a credit balance of £3,910 dwindling to £710 at the end of month 6.
- *Ongoing use* – The continuing value of the forecast is that after the first month when the actual closing balance on the bank account is known the forecast rolls forward. Column 2 becomes column 1 and so on with a new column 12 added (the 13th month in the life of the business).

Reviewing Alice's forecast for her business she will succeed in remaining within her cash limit provided that she generates new business at the projected rate and maintains her expenditure within the levels she has budgeted. However, there is almost no margin for safety and she has restricted payments to herself to a bare minimum, relying on the severance payment she received from her previous employment to cover the early months. As a self-employed person, she also benefits from payment of her telephone, utilities and motoring expenses from the business account.

Like all forecasts, much can go wrong, such as:

- *Late client payments* – The forecast is based on payment terms of 30 days from date of invoice. Hence, no revenue in month 1, when Alice's first invoice for her retainer from Gibson, Granger & Halliday is raised. All other revenue, including re-invoiced services from subcontractors is forecast on the same basis. If only all debtors paid on time. (Take on board my advice on debtor collection in the section below.)

- *Payments to creditors* – Some expenditure items cannot be delayed: bank charges and interest, staff payments, direct debits and standing orders all have to be paid on time. Try to keep your DDs and SOs to a minimum to maintain flexibility. For example, utilities and telephone bills don't have to be paid by DD; although you may be offered discounts for doing so, it is more important to have the ability to agree a delayed payment or payment schedule. You will want to pay subcontractors within their payment terms, (particularly when you start up to establish credit worthiness) but you will aim to receive payment of the re-invoiced amount before you make the corresponding payment.

- *Accidents and emergencies* – If you start off working from home, make sure that your household insurance provides sufficient cover for any foreseeable accidents on the premises. If you are operating from a separate location you will need an extra line in your cashflow forecast for insurance (monthly premiums will inevitably be made by direct debit). Some people like to include provision for contingencies in their business plans but I am not personally in favour. Contingency planning can be an excuse for sloppy budgeting and in my experience the contingency budget always manages to be spent anyway.

I shall return to the subject of cashflow forecasts in the final chapter of the book in the context of your growing business.

DAYBOOKS

Once you have registered for VAT and are keeping the required sales and purchases ledger recording all invoiced transactions in date order you will need no further record of daily activity except, perhaps, a petty cash book. Until then you can either spike your purchase orders, delivery notes, incoming invoices and statements in date order and copies of your sales invoices on another spike to be recorded weekly or monthly at your leisure (whatever that may be) online or record them daily on day books. In your early days of trading this is not too much of a chore.

OTHER ACCOUNTING RECORDS

Petty cash book
You may also find it helpful to keep a petty cash book although these days little more than taxi fares, postage stamps, cups of tea at the station and payment to the window cleaner pass through mine.

Aged debtors schedule
As your business grows and you acquire more clients/customers, it is inevitable that some invoices won't be paid on time (see below). At some stage you will find it useful to maintain an aged debtors schedule which lists all outstanding invoices and logs the amounts owing by column according to date of issue e.g. current, 30 days, 60 days and older. (Among our four examples, Simon's Case C distribution business and, maybe, Alice's PR business by the end of its second year will probably keep a schedule).

Stock records
For companies engaged in manufacturing or distribution, it is essential that you maintain stock records from the outset, usually in digital format.

Capital goods register

By definition manufacturers will have expensive capital equipment and nearly all businesses will have some items such as cars, vans and office equipment. For the preparation of profit and loss accounts and balance sheets you will need to quantify depreciation charges and written down values in their first years.

You will need the same data to calculate your eligible claims for capital allowances when filing your annual tax return, even when you are a sole trader like Fred and Alice in her first year.

DEBTOR MANAGEMENT

It all begins with your terms of business. Be very clear in advising clients and non-cash customers of your payment terms - 30 days net or a shorter period if you dare for electronic payment. Notice of payment and other critical terms, such as retention of product ownership until payment is received or copyright and risk liability limitation are best given on every quotation, order acknowledgment, invoice and statement. Technically, it is open to the client when placing an order or acknowledging receipt of goods to state their terms of business, which may differ materially from yours and, in law, the last recorded terms probably take precedence. However, in any "battle of terms" it is important to show consistency and probably your invoice will be the last relevant document.

Most clients will play fair although you may have to call their accounts departments when payment is not made on time and that can be a tiresome and time-consuming activity. It may be that the client with whom you deal has not passed on the invoice to their sales ledger department in which case you can email another copy and it will help if the original order was given an order number which you can quote.

Therefore, include a box on your order form for a number to be entered when the order is placed.

Collections from some clients, usually larger firms and companies, can be more difficult. There are two ploys which are commonly used to delay payment:

- *Supplier authorisation* – You are required to register as an accredited supplier after identity and credit checks as a part of the client's security or corporate governance policies for *bona fide* verification. The process is unavoidable; if you suspect that such a policy is in place, ask for the qualification documents as soon as your offer is accepted, for completion online.
- *Computerised invoice run* – The client's accounts department has scheduled computer runs to process invoice payments (usually monthly at month-ends). This is a good argument for specifying 15 days payment on invoices in order to improve the odds of qualifying for an early invoice run.

COMPUTERISED ACCOUNTING

There are now a number of competitively priced software packages available for electronic bookkeeping, such as the platforms offered by market leaders Xero and Quickbook, which perform the complete job or a range of task specific packages from Sage who also provide complete platforms. Purchasing accounting software piecemeal is probably a false economy. My advice is to opt for a comprehensive platform, even if you won't use all the features immediately. The features to look for from all good electronic packages are:

- Keep accurate records of your customers and suppliers.
- Reconcile your books with your online bank accounts automatically.

- Manage VAT, tax and NI including completion of your VAT returns.
- Produce your annual accounts and end-of-year reports readily.
- Highlight late payments and reduce the risk of bad debts.
- Run your payroll reliably.
- Track your credit card payments and record cash sales
- Identify which customers and products are the most and least profitable.
- Record and manage your stock levels.

As an example of good practice, the Xero platform satisfies these requirements and provides the following information in depth:

1. A dashboard showing the up to date status of:
   * bank account
   * amounts owing to you
   * bills you need to pay
   * petty cash account

2. Reports from and to whatever dates you select with comparative numbers for year to date, previous 3 months or previous years for each of:
   * profit and loss account
   * balance sheet
   * cash summary
   * aged receivables
   * aged payables
   * VAT returns

The platform also stores contact data for all customers and suppliers with their email addresses. You are enabled to see in detail exactly where your business stands at any date in the month, helping you to take a view on the current month-end results and any urgent action needed to meet and surpass forecasts.

The majority of online accounting services store data on the cloud (giant virtual online servers) but as it is key financial data, it may be prudent to ensure you have a back-up available should there be issues accessing the cloud storage at any point.

TAXATION AND TAX PLANNING

When starting your business there are two levels at which you should plan your taxation strategy: personal taxes and corporate taxes. If you are like me, you will focus on the personal element first. As the business grows and becomes profitable the balance of attention will shift towards corporate tax planning. However, so long as the business remains yours, your personal advantage is paramount.

For your start-up, as already discussed in Chapter 3, the first decision is whether to operate as a sole trader for the first year or longer or to incorporate from the outset. Setting aside the risk issues of non-incorporation, I will now attempt to clarify the comparative tax advantages from the business owner's point of view.

You are entitled to take advantage of every opportunity that the law allows for reducing the burden of taxation. Charting the optimum course is necessarily complex and, if you are confused or in any doubt after reading the sections that follow, you should take professional advice.

TAXATION AS A SOLE TRADER

Even if your new business hits the ground running, it is likely to run at a loss for a period. It is often possible for a sole trader/partnership to set off early losses against other personal income. A company's losses may be carried forward but no set-off is possible.

As an individual you are subject to income tax with the tax year running from 6 April in one year to 5 April in the next year and this was the basis for the timing advice given in Chapter 3 to set the financial year end for your business as 30 April in order to stretch the period for reporting your accounts as far as possible. However, if you start your business, for example, on 1 September 2018, the accounts for your first financial year of only 7 months would not be due for reporting until late 2020 as a part of your self-assessment tax return for the year ended 5 April 2020. Therefore, you would lose any opportunity to set off this trading loss against any personal income for the year ended 5 April 2019 and to reclaim tax already paid on income from your previous employment. In theory, you could change your financial year end from 31 March to 30 April after the first year but it is doubtful that HMRC would allow you to have your cake and eat it. You will have to take a view on the balance of advantage in your case.

The current UK rates of income tax for the year ending 5 April 2019 are:

		%
Basic rate	£1 to £34,500	20
Higher rate	£34,501 to £150,000	42
Additional rate	£150,001 and over	45

The Scottish rates are more graduated, ranging from a 19% starter rate to 41% higher rate and a top rate of 46%.

Importantly, the application of the UK basic rate is mitigated by personal income tax allowances which apply to incomes up to £100,000. For the current income tax year the universal allowance, regardless of age, is £11,850 which means that you won't have to pay income tax on the profits of your business up to that amount unless you have other taxable income to which the allowance is applied for offset.

Reviewing this in the context of Figure 5.1 and Alice's planned drawings for herself we can see that she would probably pay no tax on her first 12 months' trading for which a small loss is forecast after the £16,000 she intends to draw, sufficient to offset the taxable balance of £4,150 on her drawings.

In the worked example, Alice pays her administrative assistant Agatha a total of £6,750 in fees so that she is self-employed and no provision for PAYE is required. And in Fred's case, since his back-up is his wife Nora who doesn't receive other income, he can pay her up to £11,850 without either of them incurring a tax liability so that as his home maintenance services prosper, they will be able to earn £23,700 tax free together.

Nor should we ignore the tax reducing benefits of locating your business in your home. Provided that you are not greedy the tax inspector will apply tests of reasonableness to the amounts which you claim as business expenses from your home overheads and motoring expenses. For example if you are using 30% of your living area as your offices that would be a reasonable percentage to apply to the total cost of utilities, whereas up to 80% of IT and motoring expenses including depreciation might be acceptable if your motor vehicle is used mainly for business. Applying those ratios to the expenditure forecasts in Figure 5.1, £538 of heating and lighting costs, £568 of telephone and internet charges and £1,996 of motoring expenses could be entered as business expenditure, a total of £3,102 towards reducing your business profit and income tax liability.

Against these opportunities, the self-employed are liable for Class 2 and Class 4 national insurance contributions. The current 2018/19 flat weekly rate for Class 2 contributions is £2.95 with exemption for those earning less than £6,025 annually. The contributor is entitled to basic retirement pension, incapacity benefit, widows benefit and maternity allowance. Class 4 contributions, to which no specific benefits are attached, are calculated at 9% of profit above £8,424 up to £46,350 and 2% thereafter.

Treatment of losses

As a self-employed person you have the option of using the losses of your business to offset other taxable income so as to reduce your personal liability to tax in the same tax year and, where income tax has been deducted at source, to reclaim tax already paid. Alternatively, you may carry forward all or a part of your trading loss to the next tax year to offset against future profits and in some cases carry the loss back to previous years.

Timing of payments

Under self-assessment, half-yearly payments of income tax and National Insurance (NI) are due on 31 January and 31 July, based on the previous year's figures, with any balancing adjustment shown in the tax return and payable or repayable on the following 31 January.

Partnership losses

Individual partners are entitled to claim their shares of trading losses independently. Each partner may decide either to set his/her share of losses against other current income in the same tax year, carry the share of losses forward or, sometimes, carry back in the case of new partners.

For sole traders, you will find most of the 2018/19 tax facts that you might need on the moorepay tax fact card at https://www.moorepay.co.uk.

CORPORATE TAXATION

Once you incorporate your business taxation issues multiply and there are four distinct areas where the company has unavoidable obligations and liability:

- Company liabilities for taxation (PAYE) and NI in respect of employees
- Pension contributions
- Value added tax (VAT)
- Corporation tax

PAYE and NI

Staff who are employed as consultants are considered as non-salaried and carry no liability for the company to deduct PAYE or to make NI or pension contributions, provided that payments to an individual consultant do not exceed the current year's personal income tax allowance.

Payments to directors are liable to PAYE, either payable by the company or by the director, depending on whether they are salaried payments or invoiced management fees. The stratagem of setting up a 'personal services' company for a highly paid employee to which payment is made as fees without PAYE deductions has been prevalent (for example, among some TV presenters and entertainers earning six figure salaries). This practice is now regarded by HMRC as a device to evade tax if the service company has no other source of income, and PAYE will then be levied against the individual.

Salaried employees normally bring with them a tax code when they join the company which determines the precise amount to be deducted by the new employer from gross salary each month according to tax tables published by HMRC. Individual tax codes are reviewed and amended every financial year and notified to the employer together with an amended set of tax tables. The employer has responsibility for making the correct deductions from monthly salaries and remitting the total amount of PAYE tax deducted to HMRC.

The monthly payroll is a tedious administrative task which you will want to mechanise or subcontract out to a reputable payroll service. Interestingly, when computers were first employed as business tools, management of the payroll was very often the first accounting task for which software programmes were assigned. Management of the sales ledger and accounts receivable, which are more relevant to sustaining cashflow, took second place.

Pension contributions
Larger companies, possibly your previous employer, usually have their own pension schemes to which both the company and the individual employee make contributions.

Employee contributions are deducted from monthly salary, collected via the payroll and then paid into the pension fund together with the employer's contribution. Tax relief on employee contributions is allowed up to £40,000 per annum and in many schemes the employee can elect to top up his/her contributions to this level from the lesser monthly contributions that the company scheme requires. Tapered annual allowances are also available to high earners (those earning more than £150,000 a year including pension contributions) but these provisions are hardly relevant to you as a start-up company director.

Of greater relevance to small companies is the national Auto Enrolment Pension Scheme to which all companies without a scheme of their own must now subscribe. For the 2018/19 tax year minimum combined employer/employee contributions are 5% of gross salaries of which the employer minimum is 2%. All employees have the right to choose a pension scheme to which their employer must contribute and this scheme offers a practical option to a bespoke scheme with the balance of contributions between employer and employees negotiable.

VAT
I have included VAT under corporate taxes although the regulations apply to all businesses including sole traders and partnerships. There is the same obligation to register your VAT taxable turnover if the total of everything sold that isn't VAT exempt exceeds the current threshold of £85,000:

- In a 12 month period; or
- When you expect to go over the threshold in a single 30 day period.

Currently, you also have to register if you only sell goods or services that are exempt from VAT or "out of scope" but you buy more than £85,000 of goods from EU VAT-registered suppliers; and you may have to register for VAT if you take over a business that is already registered.

You can apply for an exception if you believe that your taxable turnover won't exceed the de-registration threshold of £83,000 in the next 12 months. Also, there is no threshold if neither you nor your business is based in the UK.

The standard rate of VAT since 4 January 2011 is 20%. Some things are exempt from VAT such as postage stamps, financial and property transactions and the services provided by charities. There are reduced and zero rates applicable as follows:

- Standard rate of 5% – some goods and services, in particular home energy
- Zero rate of 0% – other goods and services, for instance food, children's clothes and printed books

Generally, you must submit a VAT Return to HMRC every 3 months, known as "the accounting period" within 7 days of the period end. There is a VAT Annual Accounting Scheme for which some larger companies may be eligible but not your start-up. You can submit your VAT Return online or by mail but you must pay VAT owing electronically either through direct debit or internet banking. As advised earlier in this chapter it is important to integrate your VAT data records within your general accounting system; Xero and Quickbook enable you to do so.

Most start-up businesses invoice more VAT on the sale of their goods and services than they pay on their purchases of goods and services so that there is a temporary benefit to cashflow, assuming that receivables are collected on time and payables no faster than receivables. There is a trap, therefore, into which growing businesses may fall; if you do not maintain a separate VAT bank account, it is all too easy to spend the VAT collected on the day-to-day cash demands of the business so that you have difficulty in paying outstanding VAT at the end of the accounting period.

Corporation tax
Over recent years the rate of corporation tax on the profits of UK companies has been reduced steadily and now stands at 19%. Taxable "profits" are defined as net income after deduction of allowable expenses and chargeable gains in each financial year of the company. Corporate capital gains are charged at the same 19% rate.

Allowable expenses include capital allowances on plant, business equipment and motor vehicles to provide for depreciation with the rates determined by the Treasury in the Chancellor's annual budget; they include provision for early write-downs on new equipment, other than motor cars, in order to encourage investment. The details of current annual investment and write down allowances are beyond the scope of this chapter but you will find information online or through your accountant.

BALANCING BENEFITS

As you near the end of this somewhat dense chapter of information, this a good time to re-evaluate the relative advantages to the business owner of remaining a sole trader versus incorporation. In terms of risk limitation, the limited company has the clear advantage of removing personal liability for the creditors of the company beyond the statutory responsibilities of a company director. In terms of personal tax liability, the balance of benefit is more complex.

Let's assume that in either case you are employed by the business and that you don't have other taxable income against which your personal allowances could be offset. Therefore, you will each be paying income tax at 20% on the next £22,650 up to £34,500 (i.e. £4,530) under either structure, as of 2018.

After that, up to £150,000 (an unlikely level for the owner/director of any business in its early years) you will pay 40% on your profit or salary. If you choose to operate as a limited company you have the option of paying yourself dividends from company profits after deduction of corporation tax at 19% which are then taxable in your hands at the higher personal tax rate of 45%. Unless there are other shareholders involved who will expect a share of profits by way of dividend you are better off paying more salary, reducing the company's corporation tax bill and accumulating residual profits to reserves.

There is one wrinkle to the calculation: there are taxable benefits you may receive from the company as an employee such as health insurance, membership of clubs and the use of a company car. The latter is complicated and you should check carefully yourself the value of the benefit which HMRC will assess to be subject to income tax according to the vehicle you have chosen. Again, the advantage may lie with those who use their own car as a sole trader who are able to claim, say 80% of all costs, as an allowable business expense.

At the end of the day no tax regime suits everyone best. As a well-known eighteenth century parliamentarian succinctly commented:

"To tax and to please, no more than to love and be wise, is not given to men"

– *Edmund Burke (1779-1797)*

6

GOING FOR GROWTH

"Que sera, sera
Whatever will be, will be;
The future's not ours to see.
Que sera, sera
What will be, will be"

– *J Livingston & Ray Evans (1956)*

THINKING AHEAD

So, you've started your business and survived the first year, more or less in line with your business plan. You may be tempted to heave a sigh of relief and continue on your way, enjoying your freedom and in the expectation of modest growth. However, life is not like that and what may be calm waters now are almost certain to turn choppy at some time in the short to medium-term future. Even, if you are blessed with a relatively smooth passage for the first few years, you would be foolish to adopt the philosophy of the opening lyrics to this chapter, sung famously by Doris Day in Alfred Hitchcock's 1956 makeover of his *The Man Who Knew Too Much*. Indeed, if you are familiar with the movie, it is unlikely that Doris Day and her screen husband James Stewart would have recovered their kidnapped son had they adopted this *laissez faire* attitude.

The theme of this chapter, based again on a half century's business experience, is that entrepreneur's and company directors with modest ambitions seldom succeed long term. Business owners and managers who aim to keep their enterprises at a level of activity which satisfies their personal income and lifestyle requirements by repeating each year what they have done in previous years are unlikely to prosper. There are two laws of business dynamics which I have found to be invariably true:

- *Businesses that aim to stay the same will fall into decline.*
- *Businesses that budget for a loss will make a loss, probably more than expected.*

Why should these laws reflect reality? The reasons are simple. First, business conditions and markets for products and services change constantly and innovation can be disruptive as well as beneficial for those trying to surf the wave of change. And, even when the likely impact of innovation is perceived, the pace of change is seldom appreciated. Two recent and current examples spring to mind:

- The fall-out from online shopping on traditional retail outlets.
- The uncertainty of Brexit outcomes – probably negative in the short and medium term – with a dampening of the economy in the meantime.

The second reason is more psychological. Managements focused on preserving the *status quo* are, almost by definition, casting themselves as counter-entrepreneurial. And, as we shall discuss later in this chapter, over-conservative enterprises make themselves more vulnerable to being taken over as well as competition.

The converse to my two laws of business also tends to hold good:

- *Businesses that adopt a growth strategy will maintain their prosperity long-term, even if they fall short of their growth targets.*

Of course, going for growth is not intended as an incitement to abandon prudence. I am not advocating recklessness and I have already drawn attention to the perils of overtrading in Chapter 5 – *Managing cashflow*. The emphasis is on "sustainable growth" rather than a headlong flight into ill-judged expansion. The trials and tribulations of at least two successful TV chefs who have plunged into the development of signature restaurant chains, both in the UK and then internationally, are an object lessons for start-up entrepreneurs.

Therefore, the themes of this chapter are: how to achieve sustainable growth and your long-terms aims and how to capitalise on your success when you get there.

ORGANIC GROWTH VS GROWTH BY ACQUISITION

There are two paths to sustainable growth: organic growth and growth by acquisition. They are not mutually exclusive. Organic growth is achieved through profitable internal expansion: increasing turnover by enhancing your product or service range, expanding your customer base within current markets, or extending the sales territory you serve. The alternative approach is to buy other companies with complementary businesses which will extend the depth and breadth of your business immediately. If an essential element of your personal game plan is to keep shareholder control in the hands of your family and yourself, the latter strategy needs to be pursued with caution. Be mindful that you will almost certainly have to fund your acquisition programme, wholly or in part, by the issue of new shares in your company which may dilute your shareholding to the point that you no longer hold a majority of the shares.

In all cases, I recommend that you focus on organic growth first. In doing so you will have to face up to the management issues which abound as your operations and organisation expand up to and beyond the point where "small is no longer beautiful". The problem areas will include:

- Additional working capital
- Recruitment and employment
- IT and data management
- Sales and customer relations management (CRM)
- Marketing (including social media)
- Facilities and equipment
- Corporate governance

Detailed study of these important management issues is beyond the scope of this book. What I shall try to do in the sections that follow is to identify the key elements of each topic to which business owners should pay attention. As illustrations, I will relate each topic, where appropriate, to the four Cases first introduced in chapter one.

A basic reason for focusing on organic development is that this is the best way to develop your own experience and expertise as a general manager, which you will certainly need before taking to the acquisition trail. In my youth, it was quite common for entrepreneurs to acquire control of quoted 'shell' companies (old companies with little or only nominal current activity listed on a stock exchange), either by purchasing a significant existing shareholding for cash or by backing their own small company into the shell in exchange for new shares. These entrepreneurs, usually with a City background, had little if any experience of managing the day to day affairs of a service or manufacturing company or in recruiting line management with the necessary skills. Control of most of these former shell companies soon passed into the hands of larger companies, with the original entrepreneurs happily selling on and cashing in their chips, or, less happily, the businesses perished to the benefit of no-one, including creditors and employees.

In those days, many of the shell companies were listed on the regional stock exchanges, such as those in Birmingham, Manchester and Liverpool, which no longer exist, rather than London. Today, there may be some shells lingering on the AIM market of the London Stock Exchange but they are few and far between; however, the lack of management skills and experience persists among many of the investment bankers who inhabit venture capital and private equity boutiques for unlisted private companies. We will return to the perils of engaging with them in sections of the next and final chapter related to funding for acquisitions.

ADDITIONAL WORKING CAPITAL

Ideally, you will be able to generate sufficient cashflow from growing your original business to fund additional organic growth from the new activity as defined above. However, the reality is that organic business growth is not a steadily onward flowing incremental progression. At each major step in the journey, there is likely to be a need to take on additional overheads or capital expenditure before gaining an additional revenue stream. Rather like the "feast or famine" phenomenon noted in Chapter 2 in relation to planning the cashflow needs for your start-up, organic growth via expansion of your product range or services, or by venturing into new markets, is an exercise in staircase climbing – laying out additional expenditure to gain the next revenue riser.

Bank finance
If you are running your business well and fulfilling all obligations to your bank in respect of your accounts, your present bank will hopefully support your expansion.

As before, agreement to provide increased facilities will depend on the quality of the further business plan you now present. Back, therefore, to the detailed planning processes of Chapter 2 – with a difference. This time, you will be expected to report on financial results to date: filed accounts for previous financial years and a forecast for the current year's profit/loss, as well as forecasts for two or three years ahead. Once again the cashflow forecasts are fundamental.

For current year reporting, the format that I like best for internal purposes is a spreadsheet in Excel format with the following column headings:

Income/expenditure   Budget   Y/E estimate   Variance   Notes

The column items should include each significant item of income and expenditure (especially those which relate to the increased funding requirements) together with the usual subtotals for revenue, direct costs, gross profit, indirect expenses and net operating profit. When translating into cashflow projections, substitute revenue for income, adjust for the correct timings of receipts and payments and add lines for cashflow and capital expenditure.

Note that I have introduced columns for "estimated year-end" and "variance", as well as "budget". When using internally, stick to the rule that the budget is set once only at the beginning of the financial year and may not be altered. There is value in reporting the current year-end forecast and analysing variances; we have adopted this format at the

Oxfordshire charity of which I am President where much of the activity does not generate revenue and Trustees need to monitor any slippage in the bi-monthly accounts.

If the variances between budget and year-end estimate are too great or cannot be explained satisfactorily in the notes, you may not wish to include the budget and variance columns in the spreadsheets that you submit to the bank. However, the more sophisticated form of current year reporting signals that yours is a mature business under tight control and, if they are in good shape, may help to impress the bank favourably.

If the application to your bank fails, you need to know why in as much detail as possible. It may be that there is some flaw in your presentation or a reasonable doubt that your expansion plans are sound. Either way, you need to take on board all criticism and reservations and to adjust your presentation before moving on and applying to another bank.

Other sources of finance
Aside from asset finance to support capital expenditure on buildings or equipment (such as office premises for Alice's Case A PR agency) the alternative forms of debt finance identified in Chapter 4 are not really applicable for supporting organic business growth.

When Simon's Case C business expands into exports, he will probably be able to arrange a separate revolving credit facility to release cash against customers' letters of credit through UK Export Finance, the UK's government backed export credit agency, and/or his bank.

Stage 2 grants may be available to companies that have already received stage 1 funding from Innovate UK for technical feasibility studies or industrial research and can report successful outcomes from their start-ups, but these businesses are in a minority. In our own Case D of the IP transactions platform, the project never reached Stage 2 because it was unable to secure registrations from IP holders and potential buyers to confirm proof of concept.

Equity and structured finance are the most likely sources of financial support for acquisitions, to be discussed later, but should be avoided, if possible, to fund organic growth. For those who have successfully raised funding for their start-ups through crowdfunding, it may be possible to return to the same investor base for a second tranche. However, that will involve a further dilution of founders' equity although their shares should now be premium-priced.

RECRUITMENT AND EMPLOYMENT

Recruitment
Like all four of our exemplars, your business will require the recruitment of additional staff as it grows and there are a variety of ways to find good candidates. Before you start advertising or engaging with a recruitment agency, the first step is to write a job description to clarify both in your mind and to those who may help you what you are looking for from candidates. This is no easy task for small businesses which are looking for all members of staff to have some multi-functional capability and the starting point is to make an honest assessment of your own talents and shortcomings. There will be few, if any, areas of the business in which you have no part to play including tiresome tasks, such as bookkeeping or customer service. It will always be essential that you remain involved in cashflow management and in keeping a finger on the pulse of customer satisfaction and service standards.

The full job description may be used in the interview process and as an attachment to the letter of employment, once you have a chosen candidate, and the key points will be featured in the recruitment advertisement. The basic details to be included in any advertisement are:

- Job title
- Location

- Key duties and responsibilities, in brief
- Qualifications, skills and experience required
- Summary of salary and benefits
- Deadlines for applications and how they are to be made

Some companies are reluctant to quote salary, either because they don't want other staff members to compare how much their employer is prepared to pay with what they are paid themselves or because they hope to pick up someone on the cheap. Whatever the reason, withholding salary definition is a mistake; it will reduce the number of replies you can expect to be submitted.

Take care that the wording of the advertisement does not offend against any piece of discrimination legislation, such as age, gender equality or ethnicity. The same applies to letters and emails to unsuccessful candidates, both those who are discarded after reviewing their applications without interview and to those who are rejected post-interview.

Your choice of recruitment media will be determined, in part, by the seniority of the position and job responsibilities. In all cases ask for a written application before interviewing – not just written testimonials but something in the candidate's own words explaining why he/she is applying and is suitable for the job, usually in the form of a cover letter.

Recruitment media include: your own website, trade or magazine advertisement pages, recruitment agencies and, for the most senior positions (not likely until you have built a mature business), national media and executive search. Less formally, trawl your own networks and those of friends and colleagues whose opinions you value to identify promising candidates whom you may approach directly.

Interview and selection
Again, the seniority of the post or complexity of the skill set that you demand will affect the interview process: length of interview and whether or not you will select a

candidate after first interview or a second and final set of interviews. Interviewing is itself an acquired skill and you need to maintain a 'level playing field' throughout the process. This involves furnishing all interviewees with the full job description before you meet them and developing an interview structure that you follow consistently. When you are making an appointment in a field where you have little or no expertise or experience yourself, it makes sense to co-opt a second interviewer who is proficient where you are not, e.g. an IT officer or digital marketing manager. Your co-interviewer need not be a member of your team; someone whose judgment and experience you respect from outside the company may be better. In any case, there is safety in numbers and you are more likely to make a sound decision with the backup of at least one second opinion. First impressions are always important but guard against making your mind up in the first minute or so. Appointments made on the basis of 'gut feeling' alone are not often successful. And that applies also to appointments made following personal introduction.

As to the interview structure, avoid including questions which can be answered with a simple 'Yes' or 'No'. You want to draw out candidates and to hear them speak about themselves and why they think they can do the job well. Questions such as 'What have been the biggest problems in your current/last job?' are good. All questions which appear to be discriminatory on grounds of sex, race or disability (including age) are strictly off limits and could give rise to a claim against you.

At the end of the interview invite candidates to ask any questions they may have about the job or the company; explain what will happen next and when they may expect to hear the outcome. Be sure to confirm that you have a minimum of two references that are neither friends nor family whom you may telephone if your selection is favourable.

Publicity has been given recently to the application of Artificial Intelligence (AI) to recruitment interviewing online as a substitute for face to face interviews. Intuitively, this sounds like a bad idea as there is no substitute to 'seeing the whites of their eyes' and the physical impressions that candidates make in the flesh. Neither skype nor video-conferencing are fully satisfactory in forming accurate impressions. One can see that AI techniques could be helpful in weeding out unsuitable candidates to form a 'long list' for interview when the job advertised attracts dozens of applicants (as for Civil Service appointments where written applications include some rudimentary psychometric testing) but there is no place for this 'spanner' in your recruitment toolkit.

Making an offer of employment
Having made your selection, often an initial call is best but do not leave the candidate of choice waiting for longer than you have to before making a conditional job offer in writing. It is a good idea to prepare yourself with a standard letter of offer before starting the recruitment process which you can use as a template for future recruitments.

As a minimum the job offer should contain:

- The job title
- who to report to
- Conditions of the offer:
    * provision of satisfactory references
    * a probationary period of employment
    * satisfactory completion of induction procedures
    * medical fitness to work.
- Job location
- Details of remuneration (salary or wages and bonus arrangements), payment intervals and annual review date
- Any significant benefits (such as health insurance, company car or mileage allowance)
- Pension arrangements

- Hours of work
- Holiday entitlements
- The starting date
- Notice period
- Acceptance procedure

The probationary period of employment (typically 3-6 months) is particularly important. In the event that the appointment does not work out and you decide to terminate employment, it reduces to a minimum the possibility of the ex-employee making a claim for wrongful dismissal which could be taken to an employment tribunal.

References are important too. I find written references less helpful than telephone conversations with referees. Aside from the faint possibility of fraud, those giving references in writing will hesitate to express any doubts or reservations or make too strong a recommendation for fear of come-backs in the event that the appointment is a disaster. Therefore, the written reference is likely to be anodyne. Telephone references with answers to specific questions related to character and performance are usually more informative.

Contracts of employment
As soon as the appointee accepts an offer of employment for pay a contract is created. The term 'employee' now encompasses 'workers' and may include certain types of self-employment. Limited legal protection is also given to qualifying temporary workers. The recent case of self-employed Uber taxi drivers who claimed successfully that they had worker status confirms how far workers' rights have now been extended. An offer of employment can be verbal or written in express or implied terms, which is why it is important that your job offers should be specific, detailed and in writing with both offer and acceptance signed.

Since the Employment Rights Act of 1996, all employers have been obliged to provide their employees within two months of commencement with a written statement of employment particulars based on the information included in the letter of offer for which I have listed the terms recommended above. Failure to provide the required details on time may enable a disgruntled employee to complain to the Employment Tribunal which can award two to four weeks' pay. (A week's pay in 2017 was capped at £489, subject to annual review on 6 April).

In nearly all cases today you will need to provide a written contract of employment that in addition to the above should include:

- Grievance and disciplinary procedures
- Health and safety provisions
- Flexible working policies
- General employment practices such as data confidentiality, email and internet use

You need to be aware of, and may choose to circulate, staff with the minimum statutory provisions, many of which implement European directives from the EC and which are followed by other EU members. Some of these provisions will be included in the contract. Others, which cannot be overridden, include:

- National minimum wage, reviewed annually
- Working time regulations
- Statutory sick pay reviewed annually
- Minimum legal notice periods (one week after one month for up to two years; two weeks after two years, continuous employment plus an additional week for each further year up to a maximum of 12 weeks.)
- Employers' liability insurance
- Maternity leave, paternal and shared parental leave
- Time off to care for dependants
- Whistleblowing.

You also need to check that you are fully aware of the equality provisions introduced in the UK Equality Act 2010 which outlaw discrimination on a multitude of grounds. These can easily trip up employers as a friend of mine found out recently. When chairing an AGM, he referred light heartedly to the efforts of the Company Secretary in encouraging attendance as 'sheepdogging', to which they took exception. (I am still not entirely clear whether the protest was on their own behalf or for the canine sub-species).

The written statement of employment can be drafted by yourself internally (templates are available online). For the more formal contract, you should take advice from a solicitor who can help generate a template that can be amended for all future employees. Note: if you get the initial contract wrong and decide to give notice in the future, it could be expensive.

This section of the chapter may be more detailed than you need now and is longer than I originally intended. However, staff relations are so important to the smooth running of a company that you need no distraction from concentrating on growing the business.

INFORMATION AND COMMUNICATIONS TECHNOLOGY (ICT) AND DATA MANAGEMENT

The explosion in ICT over the past 30 years has completely changed the way in which we do business worldwide. Following the invention of Tim Berners-Lee's World Wide Web and the first communication between server and Hypernet Transfer Protocol (HTT) client in 1989, emails have displaced letter-writing and are often preferred over telephone calling, the fax has become redundant when signed business documents are scanned in and sent as email attachments and time intervals in developing new business and interacting with suppliers and customers have collapsed as same day response has eclipsed 'by return of post'.

Online banking has facilitated the rapid completion of transactions and helped bank customers to manage their cashflows more efficiently from PC, smartphone or tablet. Other innovations in telecommunication, not least the evolution of the mobile phone into a portable business platform, have enabled business to be conducted outside the office, on the move and between time zones at any time of day or night. Much business travel has become a matter of choice rather than necessity with communication flowing freely between service provider and client, or between supplier and customer.

The same is true of adult education, with business courses and more formal post graduate diplomas and degrees delivered as distance learning. All of these tools are available to small business owners and greatly enhance their ability to grow their businesses by harnessing remote communication.

Data collection and storage have become less irksome tasks; farewell to the filing cabinet, store securely on the Cloud instead. And as a start-up, you have the opportunity to take advantage of all the technology and modern methods of communication and, by deploying them, to run your business efficiently.

Data analytics are a growing field for the application of AI and I will return to this topic below in relation to customer relations management and marketing. Meantime, they are an integral part of the computerised accounting software available from Xero, Quickbook, Sage or others which I commended in Chapter 5. If you have not yet bought into one of them, now is the time while you are in expansion mode and I urge you to do so before the requirements of maintaining a healthy business swing back to internal management and administration.

As a footnote to this section, have in mind the early recruitment of a well-trained and talented ITC specialist if you envisage extensive use of data analytics and of sales and marketing strategies dependent on use of the internet and social media. The right appointee can take control of all ITC activity including data and cybersecurity, website development and digital marketing.

SALES AND CUSTOMER RELATIONS MANAGEMENT (CRM)

The sharp end of your drive for business growth is sales and CRM activity. I am commenting on CRM which is vital to repeat business first before addressing marketing and sales to new customers and clients. Of our four cases only Simon's Case C is more focused on primary sales for the reason that he is unlikely to sell a second remote controlled fuel tank cap (his core product) to the same customer twice in the foreseeable future.

For Fred's Case B home maintenance service and Alice's Case A public relations firm customer relations are crucial in maintaining steady flows of business based on customer loyalty. Good ongoing customer relations with IP transactions members would also have been a key factor in maintaining membership income for Case D. Reliance on successfully completed sales and purchases at highly infrequent intervals would not have been sufficient to sustain membership renewals.

Data analytics can certainly help you to understand your customer's behaviour patterns, needs and levels of satisfaction if your records are digitalised so that their experience of working with you and vice versa are recorded and posted online rather than consigned to hard copy files. Therefore, you can take advantage of the technology tools described above to provide high quality contact and to convert first-time customers into regulars. But personal contact is essential for both Alice and Fred and that involves more than communication via social media or one-to-one emailing.

Speaking as a consumer, I find it greatly irritating to be

badgered by Facebook, Twitter and repeated emails from people whose offers of service I have rejected or with whom I don't want to be in contact. Mature businesses will probably succumb to these practices in time but start-ups should cultivate more personalised relationships with friendly and well-briefed staff communicating primarily by telephone. Having said that, cold telephone calling can be equally offensive and we'll return to that topic in the context of marketing.

Using digitalised customer data to optimum effect requires training and customer relations experience grounded in data analysis is a desirable skill to look for when recruiting. Fred's business started out with no back-office staff other than his wife, who took advantage of the low cost ITC and computer training courses on offer from their local authority and signed up to several. The available training programmes also helped her to manage the company's accounting using Sage software.

On a cautionary note, watch out for new regulatory and compliance demands which may interrupt 'business-as-usual' practices. You need to respond to such changes as the EU's General Data Protection Regulations (GDPR), which came into force on 18 May 2018, efficiently and effectively. GDPR applies to all enterprises and organisations regardless of activity and size. For start-ups they involve seeking explicit or implicit consent to continued communication with all other enterprises and individuals with whom you are in contact. They are not too onerous to navigate but do take care. Penalties for getting it wrong are potentially severe.

MARKETING

There is a clear distinction between *internet marketing:* using some or all of the tools referred to above from:

- Emailing lists of identified potential customers;
- Promotional messages on social media, principally

Facebook, Twitter and Linkedin
- Paid advertising on Google and social media platforms
- Your own website, an open source of information about your business and its product or service offerings

And *conventional marketing:* using the tried and tested tools of yesteryear ranging from:

- Personalised letters and mail shots sent by post
- Leaflet drops via newspaper rounds
- Trade press and business directories
- National or local newspaper advertising
- Local press editorial and radio or TV coverage
- Telephone cold calling
- Speaking, advertising or networking at sponsored seminars and conferences

The route that you use for your company will be determined mainly by the nature of your business and whether you operate in a local, regional, national or even international market. The tool that is common to both approaches is your website and I must reiterate that it is worth spending money on creating a website that is both informative, visitor friendly and interactive. It is important that your homepage is sufficiently compelling to drive potential clients into clicking on to further pages which will provide the detailed information which they want and prompt them to contact you by telephone or email. For example, to be visitor friendly the architecture of your website should make it easy to move from one page to another without having to trawl back through the homepage. It is difficult to build a website that is truly innovative, but you should strive to be sufficiently striking to stand out from competitors' websites and to avoid being 'clunky'.

It is unlikely that you will have the in house skills to build a really good website and should subcontract the design and construction to a specialist. You and your marketing/ sales team can write the copy and provide direction on page contact. Alternatively, if you are using a PR agency take their advice on the text and on the provision of further page copy when the website is in use.

It is still possible to have built a professional website for less than £1,000 which could include basic interactivity such as a blog and Contact Us forms. From quite recent experience of outsourcing the construction of more sophisticated website platforms with fully bespoke functionality and intelligent built-in SEO (to ensure strong rankings on search engines) I would advise you to budget for not less than £10,000.

You also need to ensure that at least one of your staff is trained to manage the posting of new information and marketing messages on the website to keep it fresh and to handle contact enquiries. Some large companies or managed service providers, such as international IT software companies, allow contact only by email or from their websites, but generally I think it is a mistake to deny or discourage telephone contact even if your headquarters are in Silicon Valley.

So, which channels are the most appropriate for each of our four business cases? Alice needs a superior website for her PR agency which showcases her communications skills and identifies how she supports clients. However, because confidentiality and personal relationships with clients are the essence of her business, advertising the agency and use of social media are restricted to a profile on Linkedin and inviting existing contacts and people with whom she would like to meet to connect with her. Amongst the conventional marketing aids, the only tools with which she feels comfortable are non-advertising appearances in the local business press or radio/TV. Cold calling is only appropriate for contacts to whom Alice has been given introductions.

Fred is in a similar situation to Alice for his home

maintenance business and local advertising is useful and will not offend existing clients. The only online medium appropriate for his business is advertising on local business and authority websites. Among the conventional tools leaflets and small advertisements in local directories may be effective but most of his new business will come from client recommendations and networking.

Only Simon's remote control fuel cap distribution business (Case C) and Case D's transaction business are reliant on internet marketing to succeed. Simon will find trade outlets for his product through directories, attendance at trade shows and researching online for fuel oil distributors. Otherwise, the thrust of his marketing will be to generate direct sales to fuel tank owners through his website, through advertising on Google and in DIY catalogues and by publicity in the press and on TV.

The effectiveness of Google as an advertising medium is sometimes uncertain but it is beloved by big companies and advertising agencies because responses can be gauged through statistical reports showing the number of home and further page 'hits', time spent on websites and downloads. However, only actual sales provide the real proof.

FACILITIES AND EQUIPMENT

I have little to add to the advice given in previous chapters on procurement and asset funding except for a footnote on office, factory and distribution facilities. Plainly, as business expands you will need more space but be careful to retain as much flexibility as is sensible. In general, leasing is to be preferred rather than freehold purchase. It is true that real estate assets can be resold and leased back in order to make a profit or free capital but property markets are fickle and you are not a property company.

There has been a steady trend, particularly in office

space, for length of leases, and rent review and break clause intervals to be shortened. For factories and warehouses, however, where the costs of removal and transfer of equipment to new premises are considerable, plainly there is an advantage in leasing for 10 or more years with frequent break clauses and options on adjacent property to allow for expansion if the business grows rapidly.

A major factor in leasing office space has been the evolution of short-term letting opportunities for small units in refurbished and well-appointed premises in city centres by landlords such as Regus, which offers attractive packages including security services and the use of communal boardrooms for occasional meetings. For companies located in the provinces in smaller cities or out of town business centres, it should be possible to negotiate a break clause every 1-3 years in a longer fully repairing lease. Such an arrangement would suit Alice well as she plans to recruit office staff steadily after the first two years and to expand regionally.

CORPORATE GOVERNANCE

Even small companies have need to include corporate governance in their back office activity. You will already have written policies on recruitment, employment and human relations, terms of business on the reverse side of your proposals and invoices, customer management and GDPR. Without making a meal of it, you should assemble all of these into a corporate governance folder, adding to them policies on health and safety, security, the use of company intellectual property and any others of importance to your business. Responsibility for monitoring and corporate governance compliance should be assigned to a senior member of staff reporting to yourself.

TIMING

Obviously, you can't do it all at once and you will have to focus on each element in turn in whatever seems the most appropriate order as your business takes off. However, all of them are important and should be mastered before you consider looking for acquisitions. Timing, as Brutus said, is everything.

"There is a tide in the affairs of men,
Which, taken at the flood, leads to fortune;
On such a full sea we are now afloat,
And we must take the current when it serves,
Or lose our venture."

– *Julius Caesar, William Shakespeare (1564-1616)*

7

ACQUISITIONS AND ENDGAME

"Not all that tempts your wandering eyes
And heedless hearts, is lawful prize;
Not all that glisters, gold."

– Thomas Grey (1716-1771)

UNDERSTANDING THE PLAYING FIELD

Before making your first acquisition, analyse your motives.
For some the idea of growing a group of companies through
acquisition has an almost romantic aura. Certainly, a successful
acquisition is good for the ego if you pay a sensible price and the
business you are taking on goes well, but ambitions to become a
takeover tycoon are dangerous. Acquisitions are never magical,
usually involve a high degree of risk, are often traumatic and can
lead to unintended consequences. And, if your business is the
one to be acquired, the damage may be irreparable.

Let's start by clarifying a common misconception that
mergers and acquisitions are two wholly distinct species;

they are not. In a merger two companies are combined, either by one (Company A) issuing new shares to the shareholders of another company (Company B) in exchange for their shareholdings at an agreed ratio, or by forming a new holding company that issues shares to the shareholders of both companies in agreed proportions.

In an acquisition Company A purchases the shares or the assets of Company B in exchange for cash, loan stock with, perhaps, some shares or a mixture of all three. For practical purposes, the result is usually the same: the shareholders of company A become the majority owners of the combined two businesses.

The reality is that Company A shareholders are the predators, the business of Company B is the prey and Company B shareholders are often the victims. The term 'merger' is frequently applied as a euphemism for what is in practice simply a takeover. Sometimes, the term is employed to soothe the feelings of Company B's staff and former owners, particularly if arrangements are made for continuity of the previous management. I shall have more to say about different outcomes later in the chapter.

ACQUISITION MOTIVES

For now, the task is to identify what are the motives that make acquisition a health enhancing strategy for your company. The following are sound reasons for looking at acquisition opportunities:

- Access to an expanded market – either at home or internationally.
- Deeper penetration of the present market – where increased size brings economies of scale.
- Reduction or elimination of competition to achieve market domination.

- Diversification – where the addition of complementary products or services increases business with existing customers through cross-selling and spreads risk.
- Liberation of under-utilised assets.

Let's look at each of these motives in more detail in the context of the four cases to which most of this book relates. The fifth motive is not really valid for young companies seeking growth. For mature companies that have already achieved critical mass for their businesses, opportunistic asset-stripping has its place, but not at this point.

Alice's PR company (Case A)

From start-up Alice has had in mind the possibility of expanding her business based in Oxfordshire into other regional business centres within the UK – Birmingham, Leeds, Manchester and Bristol are at the top of her list. The arguments for expanding by acquisition rather than attempting to start up in each location using the experience gained from her original start-up are:

- Comparative risk: the difficulty of recruiting management talent and the requirement for additional working capital for each venture.
- Barriers to entry: challenging established, successful businesses.
- Faster rate of growth: an instant addition to group turnover and, hopefully, profit rather than a two-to-three-year time-lag before achieving incremental growth.

Similar reasoning applies to an opportunity for Alice to acquire a direct local competitor, particularly if the target has established a clientele in industry sectors or other types of organisation that Alice's company has not yet penetrated. Such an acquisition also offers the opportunity to combine office and back-office staff leading to reduced overheads.

Market domination is usually defined as more than 25% share of that market and that may be a third motive for acquisition if it gives Alice a firmer grip on her existing client base.

Diversification of services may also be a sensible motive. Alice's PR advisory role often includes recommendations to existing clients for website development work involving expenditure up to £10,000. She has several website design companies with which she works regularly and the acquisition of one of these would add to the value of her existing client business and offer opportunities to market her PR services to its own customer base.

PR and advertising go hand-in-hand but combining them in the same agency could be self-defeating since clients like to retain close control of their advertising spend and would react against a PR agency that tries to push them into spending more. Instead, they look for effective PR as a substitute for excessive advertising.

By contrast, coaching clients in presentational skills for radio, TV interviews that PR has generated and public appearances could also be a suitable business for acquisition.

Fred's home maintenance business (Case B)
Fred has configured his business case as a local supplier offering a very personal service and generating new clients by referral. For such a low overhead and price competitive business, expanding into a wider area would very likely dilute response times and service levels and therefore would be a costly mistake.

However, he always envisaged expanding the range of services that he offered from plumbing into home heating, electrical and decorating services. All such businesses operating on a similar scale to Fred on the basis of keenly priced personal services tend, like him, to value highly their independence – hardly targets for corporate acquisition. Even a limited liability partnership with more than two partners is probably not a comfortable relationship. More likely to appeal to Fred is a series of joint ventures in which each participant retains independence and is assigned responsibilities and rewards in advance. So here is a joint-venture rather than an acquisition opportunity.

Simon's remote-control security fuel tank cap (Case C)

Simon is in a different situation altogether. His business needs as wide a geographical spread as possible working through fuel oil and tank suppliers, both domestic and international. Acquisitions will play no part in his territorial expansion plans.

As a one product business, diversification may be crucial to growing the company's profitably by adding compatible products to develop a product range marketable through the same distribution chain and channels to market. He has his own new product development programme (e.g. remote-control doorlocking systems and electric blanket switches) but the acquisition of an established business supplying his target markets could be attractive even if its product range is not directly related.

Given that Simon is a newcomer to the home security market with only a few years under his belt, any acquisition could take the form of a 'reverse takeover': the backing of one business into another through an issue of sufficient new shares to give the leading party effective control of the combined business. This rather more complicated transaction involves the same basic processes as a straightforward acquisition but demands more expertise from advisers and possibly the introduction of a third-party financial investor.

The IP transaction platform (Case D)

Acquisition would have played little if any part in its development strategy. By its nature as a business operating and marketing online, Google and social media PPC advertising would have targeted a global audience. Networking with patent and trademark attorneys and agents would also have helped to extend boundaries and gain acceptance in new markets worldwide. The only diversification envisaged was into patent registration or perhaps auctions but this could have been accomplished by alliances or employing expert practitioners.

THE PROCESSES OF ACQUISITION

There are seven stages in completing an acquisition, which follow a logical sequence:

- Target identification
- Opening negotiations
- Appointing and instructing advisers
- Agreeing terms
- Due diligence
- Drafting contracts
- Exchange and completion of contracts

Before commenting on each stage in turn, prepare yourself for the amount of your time that the complete process will take and the effect that may have on your core business over a period that is likely to be longer than you expected. Make contingency plans for handling both critical and day-to-day business in your part absence; consider taking on a temporary senior staff member that you can trust for the period of disruption that may continue after completion as you complete the integration of the business you have just bought with your own.

Target identification
Maybe you will have earmarked one or two possible targets in the course of your normal business activities. Alternatively, the owner of another business may approach you either directly or through an adviser. Sometimes, you will be

approached by someone who offers to put you in touch with a potential target whom they know but do not represent. In the latter case, the adviser will be looking to you to pay for his services; remember the advice and cautionary tale of Chapter 4 in respect of using agents to raise funds. Limit your commitment to the payment of a finder's fee of not more than 5% of the purchase consideration, payable only on completion of an acquisition that they have introduced. Do not involve any finder whom you commission in negotiations following the introduction; their advice is likely to be biased towards payment of the finder's fee.

Opening negotiations
How you approach a target is a matter of judging the approach that will appeal most to the owners of the business and that best suits your personal style of communication. Generally asking "Mr Jones, I want to buy your company; would you consider selling?" is less likely to resonate than "Mr Jones, I think that combining our businesses would be good for us both; would you consider some form of alliance?" The latter approach may lead into euphemistic talk of merger, but the real nature of the relationship will soon become apparent in the course of any negotiations.

Preliminary discussions are partly a courting routine, partly to scope what the target owner wants and also an opportunity to identify any roadblocks to acquisition and major risks that might cause you to break off. Unless you are an accomplished acquisition practitioner do not enter into discussion on price or how the purchase consideration might be paid at this first stage. You may discover whether or not the present owner would want to continue working for the company, although you will not want to openly discuss that possibility now. If the business owner is receptive and you decide to go further, the best way to close the initial discussion is to agree that you will each consult your professional advisers and sign a mutual non-disclosure agreement to cover further exchange of information.

Appointing and instructing advisers

You will need both lawyers and accountants to manage the detail of your acquisition and it is wise to appoint and consult them at an early stage. It is important to select your professional advisers from firms with extensive experience of acquisition transactions. The same applies to your choice of law firm. Do not flinch from abandoning the local friendly firm of accountants or solicitors who handle your normal business transactions if they lack expertise in acquisitions. You cannot afford to be sentimental. You will be counting on your lawyers to carry out the rest of the formal due diligence process, to draft the sale and purchase agreement, plus any side agreements such as employment contracts, and to argue them all out with the vendor's solicitor at the appropriate time.

Agreeing terms

This stage is likely to be the most difficult part of the proceedings. Based on the accounting information that the vendor supplies, usually past years' accounts, current year management accounts and year-end forecasts, you have to value the shares of the company you intend to acquire, or its assets net of liabilities if you will not be purchasing the shares. The final valuation may be amended in light of the accountant's full report and due diligence, but for now you have to come up with a price that you are prepared to pay and an opening offer that will be lower.

The decision is yours but rely on your advisers to tell you what is realistic and safe. Basically, there are two ways to value an acquisition, either by reference to sustainable earnings – net profits before interest, taxation, depreciation and amortisation (EBITDA) – or on shareholders' funds – the balance sheet value of fully paid up share capital plus or minus retained earnings (negative in the case of accumulated net losses).

Ideally, you would wish to pay no more than the balance sheet value of the shares, because any additional amount will be treated as goodwill and as an intangible asset on your post-acquisition balance sheet. However, that is unlikely in the case of service companies such as Alice's PR agency targets. Much will depend on the size of the company and its trading record. You will need to inspect at least three years' accounts showing a steady record or growing profits to justify a higher price while the vendor may be keen to value their company on the basis of current year performance or a projected revenue multiple in order to try to get to a higher agreed number.

Taking a multiple of EBITDA to calculate price is really applicable only to companies with a stock market listing where comparisons can be made with the price/earnings ratios of other companies in the same field of activity. For private company valuations it is normal to value at a multiple of net profits after all charges but before taxation. The technology sector has recently skewed perception as to multiples through its headline deals where companies pay billions of dollars for organisations not yet in profit. However, outside of the bubble of Silicon Valley, for a company with a good record and a stable outlook a multiple of 3 to 4 times would usually be appropriate. If current year forecast results are to be taken into account, the purchaser might suggest a lower price with a top-up in the event that current year profits are higher. This kind of arrangement is often referred to as an 'earn out'.

From the vendor's point of view, an earn-out related to net profit is dangerous unless they are left in sole charge of the company during the period of the earn-out, and that is unlikely to be acceptable to you if you want to integrate the two businesses as soon as possible. As an alternative, the vendor's advisers may suggest that the earn-out is related to any increase in gross profit leaving you free to add to overheads or apply management charges. But that is also unsatisfactory if your intervention is likely to generate increased sales through cross-selling or improved gross margins.

You will have to navigate your way through these difficulties in the course of negotiations and there is no 'one-size-fits-all' solution. If the purchase consideration is partly or wholly in shares, any increase in consolidated group profits resulting from the acquisition will improve the value of the shares issued and may mitigate the difficulty. However, increases in the value of shares in an unlisted company are no substitute for cash in hand and a better approach to earn-out arrangements may be to offer a generous service agreement for the period of the earn-out with a cash bonus or top-up to the vendor's pension fund if targets are achieved.

Once you have reached agreement, I recommend that you produce a 'Term Sheet', subject to contract, which confirms succinctly in writing the terms agreed. This is a substitute for the more formal heads of agreement drafted by lawyers. When both parties have signed off on the Term Sheet, it is passed to the lawyers to start drafting the formal agreements.

Due Diligence

There are three elements in due diligence which are skimped at the purchaser's peril:

1. Financial Due Diligence – carried out by your accountants to examine and report on the vendor's financial accounts, forecasts, accounting systems, pension arrangements and past, pending and future tax liabilities.

2. Legal Due Diligence – carried out by your lawyers to examine any material contracts that the target company may have with third-parties, such as leases of premises and equipment, agreements with banks and suppliers, service agreements with directors and staff, other contracts of employment with staff and consultants, insurance policies, health and safety compliance and now GDPR provisions.

3. General Due Diligence – your own assessment of how the company operates, such as management capability and performance, staff skills, customer service routines, customer and supplier relationships.

(Just how much access the vendor will give you to investigate within the company will be uncertain.)

Drafting contracts

Having satisfied yourself and your advisers through due diligence that there are no unexpected obstacles, your lawyer can proceed to draft contracts. The core document will be the Purchase and Sale Agreement between your company and the vendors personally. If you are retaining management there will be one or more Service Agreements, and if you are taking on offices or other premises either owned or leased by the vendor there will be a lease or sub-lease in the name of one or other company.

Aside from setting out the detailed terms of sale and purchase, which will be more complex if consideration other than cash is involved (e.g. restrictions on the sale of new ordinary shares issued or interest payments and redemption terms in the case of preference shares or loan stock) the Purchase and Sale Agreement will include Warranties and Indemnities that the vendor is required to give as insurance against unexpected liabilities that may surface after completion.

Warranties are intended to focus the seller's mind on disclosing matters that are inconsistent with the information revealed in the due diligence process and to provide the buyer with a remedy of claiming in damages if the warranty later proves to be false and the buyer suffers consequent loss. They can be a formidable schedule and I advise you to limit them to matters that, if disclosed, would affect materially the value of the business and its future profitability. Receiving a 40-page schedule can unnerve any seller and could spoil the deal. By contrast indemnities are to protect the buyer against tax liabilities not provided for on the warranted accounts or that have not arisen yet on profits since the last balance sheet and for specific risks that have been identified such as a dispute with a former employee.

There are standard ways to limit the seller's liabilities under the warranties:

- Disclosures – A disclosure letter either from either the vendor or the vendor's lawyer to the buyer or the buyer's lawyer listing specific items in detail.
- Time limits – Within which a claim must be brought; typically two or three years for all claims other than tax for which seven years is customary.
- Financial limits – Several limits are standard: minimum limits both for individual claims and the aggregate of claims (typically around 1 per cent of the purchase consideration) below which the buyer cannot bring a claim; a cap normally equal to the consideration paid, although if the consideration for shares was nominal (e.g. the buyer repaid a substantial shareholders' loan instead) the limit should be determined by the degree of commitment or risk that the buyer is taking on.

As to the drafting of service contracts for senior members of staff who may be staying, I would urge you to be careful. In my experience, when the vendor is continuing with the company the engagement seldom lasts for more than a year. The tide of goodwill that takes you up to completion may ebb quite quickly with changes in how you wish the business to operate and your management style. If the vendor plans to retire after a year, there may be little problem; you can always resort to 'gardening leave' if relations become too strained. For other senior staff 1-2 year rolling contracts would be sensible.

Exchange and completion of contracts

Unlike property transactions, there is normally no interval between exchange of contracts and completion. After all the time and effort you and your team have put into negotiating the deal and agreeing contracts with the vendor, the completion meeting, probably at your lawyer's office when all agreements are signed, shares are transferred and the consideration paid, will happen very quickly unless there is any last minute hitch.

This is the end of the process involving professional advisers but only the starting gun for making the acquisition work.

Note: Bear in mind all the points in this chapter so far for when you come to sell your business in the future and find yourself in the role of seller.

THE MORNING AFTER

It may be that the integration of the new business is seamless but that is only likely if you were able during the period when contracts were being agreed to sit down with the management who are joining you and plan in some detail. It is more likely that there will be unease and a period of adjustment before the two parts of the business operate smoothly together.

I have found that a good way to handle this period of change is to identify someone among the team who are joining you and, after exposure to the way you run your business, appoint him/her as the champion of change to bring the rest of the team on side. This works better rather than risking conflict by doing the work yourself. It also leaves you in the position of ultimate arbiter and, if necessary, as court of appeal.

FUNDING THE ACQUISITION

It's likely that the vendor(s) will not want shares in your unlisted company in exchange for theirs and that you will not have the cash resources or a sufficient bank facility to make a wholly cash payment possible. You may be thrown back on the need to negotiate investment from a private equity fund or another investor. Time now to revisit Chapter 4 and take the discussion further.

If an investor was prepared to subscribe the amount you need for new ordinary shares in your company up to, say 30% of the issued capital you might be pleased to have a minority shareholder with financial expertise. However, that is not how private equity invests. The packages that they offer, described collectively as 'structured finance', take the form of a small investment in equity at a low share price with the greater part of the investment in the form of interest-bearing Preference Shares and/or Loan Stock. In this way their risk exposure is reduced.

Preference Shares rate as equity with the right to repayment of principal and interest in the event of liquidation ahead of Ordinary Shares. There will be provisions for redemption at a future date or dates. Often the redemption price includes a premium on the original subscription price.

Loan Stock is more often than not secured on the assets of the company with repayment at fixed intervals in tranches or in full at a future date. Interest rates on both Preference Shares and Loan Stock are usually acceptable but often they come with conversion rights which allow the holders to convert the whole or a part of their investments into new Ordinary Shares and this is where you need to be very careful. In either case, exercise of conversion rights may give the investor a bigger shareholding then you would wish and possibly the dilution of your shareholding below the 51% that you need to retain control. Once made these commitments are very difficult to undo. Make sure you take the best professional advice available.

ENDGAME

I have no more advice to give you in this book about starting and growing your business after the first acquisition except to take care to consolidate any further acquisition each time before moving on to the next.

One day an opportunity will come to sell your business

and cash in your chips. That may be sooner than you had planned or would wish; you may still have the enthusiasm to grow your business and have no incentive to sell yourself short when you see a clear way forward to increasing the value of your company and perhaps even floating on a stock exchange. You may be right, but the best advice I have ever received on this issue was from a very canny corporate lawyer and friend. He left me with two firm strictures:

- Never fall in love with your business – you can always build another.
- If someone offers you a good price for your shares but you are minded to stay involved, take 50% in cash and stay in with the rest of your holding.

I have followed that advice twice since – once with a management buyout which I led and the second with a minority shareholding in a Chinese joint venture that I set up. I have never regretted either decision.

At the end of the day, you should be able to look back and say that the all the critical decisions in your career and the responsibility for them were yours and yours alone. I leave you with familiar words from Frank Sinatra. It seems appropriate that he was referred to by his Rat Pack colleagues and friends as "Chairman of the Board".

"Regrets, I've had a few
But then again, too few to mention
I did what I had to do
And saw it through without exemption
I planned each charted course
Each careful step along the byway
And more, much more than this
I did it my way"

– Claude Francois and Jacques Revaux (1967)

LEGEND BUSINESS IS PART OF THE LEGEND TIMES GROUP

LEGEND PRESS
LEGEND BUSINESS
NEW GENERATION PUBLISHING
PAPERBOOKS

READ MORE LEGEND BUSINESS TITLES...

ISBN: 9781787197909
EBOOK: 9781787197893
PRICE: £19.99
EXTENT: 224 PAGES

THE INVESTMENT HANDBOOK

This is the handbook that consolidates all of the material that every entrepreneur needs when they are looking to raise capital. The guide is an invaluable resource for an entrepreneur or business owner, providing immediate information and contact details to access many of the world's leading business investors.

Containing valuable information about the preferred sectors that they allocate money to, along with details about their typical size of investment, allowing those looking to raise money to drill down to a more relevant target audience.

In addition to the details Directory, the handbook has chapters of advice written by experienced investment professionals, covering topics such as: What investors want in return, common mistakes (an investor's view), valuing your business, and what to do when you don't get funding.

READ MORE LEGEND BUSINESS TITLES...

ISBN: 9781785079320
EBOOK: 9781785079337
PRICE: £14.99
EXTENT: 144 PAGES

The Business Plan is an essential tool for attracting an investor's attention. They receive hundreds of plans every week and spend no more than ten minutes on each one before deciding if it is of further interest. This means that the plan needs to be a short, snappy conveying the facts about your business quickly and clearly.

This book explains how to write a plan that has the information that an investor needs to see. It shows that it is a simple process and anyone can do it, irrespective of background or prior knowledge.

Business Plans That Get Investment is a clear and comprehensive guide to writing a plan that turns those ten minutes of attention into investment.

READ MORE LEGEND BUSINESS TITLES...

ISBN: 9781789550016
EBOOK: 9781789550009
PRICE: £9.99
EXTENT: 130 PAGES

SMART SKILLS: COMMUNICATIONS

Communication isone of the most basic function in any organization. It is the process of transmitting ides, thoughts, information, opinons, and plans between various parts of an organization as well as to external customers or businesses. The essential elements to successful business communication are structure, clarity, consistency, medium and relevancy.

This book will guide you through the pitfalls and enable you to target and convey your information through software, telephone or in-person methods.

Regardless of what medium you use, effective communication ensuring your message is received clearly and is understood entirely.